Rifleman Sahib

Rifleman Sahib

The Recollections of an Officer
of the Bombay Rifles During the
Southern Mahratta Campaign,
Second Sikh War, Persian Campaign
and Indian Mutiny

E. Maude

LEONAUR

Rifleman Sahib: the Recollections of an Officer of the Bombay Rifles During the Southern Mahratta Campaign, Second Sikh War, Persian Campaign and Indian Mutiny
by E. Maude

First published under the title
Oriental Campaigns & European Furloughs

This edition has been carefully edited to remove material
with no military history content

Published by Leonaur Ltd

ISBN: 978-1-84677-478-2 (hardcover)
ISBN: 978-1-84677-477-5 (softcover)

http://www.leonaur.com

Publisher's Notes

Contents

To my dear wife, children and grandchildren
These records are affectionately dedicated

Prefatory Note

In submitting these *Memoirs of the Life of an Indian officer, from Cadet to Colonel*, to an indulgent public, I have endeavoured to depict my experiences in an unpretentious and accurate manner, avoiding the high colouring which sometimes accompanies works on *The Gorgeous East*. I trust the work may prove useful and instructive to the many young officers and others whose careers lie in India, as well as of interest to the many who have relatives and friends in that country. I hope also it may induce the general public at home to take a *more practical* interest in that wonderful country with its teeming millions, and when possible to visit it, now that railway facilities make it easy and comfortable to do so.

A noble example has been set in this respect by our gracious Sovereign, and more recently by T.R.H. the Prince and Princess of Wales, in their Indian tour, which, under the able guidance of Sir W. Lawrence, they both enjoyed, and by their gracious manner and kindly interest in the welfare of the people earned their devotion and gratitude.

E. M.
Riversdale
Bournemouth
December 1907

CHAPTER 1

I Obtain an Indian Cadetship

In the autumn of 1843 I was pursuing my studies at the High School of the Liverpool Institution (now called *Queen's College*) waiting for an Indian cadetship that had been promised me by General B., a connection of our family.

During the summer I paid visits to some relatives in the lovely Lake District, and though they were somewhat saddened by the shadow of a long farewell, I yet enjoyed myself in boating and fishing, with occasional rides and picnic excursions, etc. I had also the privilege of being introduced to some celebrities in the neighbourhood, among others to Dr. Arnold of Rugby fame, Miss Martineau, Hartley Coleridge, and last but not least the venerable poet Wordsworth, with whom I had the honour of a pleasant walk on the banks of the sparkling little river Brathay. With his best wishes, he gave me good advice about my future in India, warning me against the pernicious *brandy-pawnee* drinking, and urging me not to give in to the climate, etc.

At length, about the end of November, I received the welcome tidings that I had obtained my cadet-ship, and was directed to report myself without delay at the India House.

Accordingly, taking leave of my esteemed cousin and guardian (for whose interest in my welfare I shall ever feel grateful), as well as of my teachers and schoolfellows, and receiving their cordial good wishes, I proceeded to London, thence to Woolwich, and put up with a military relative at the Royal Artillery Barracks. Soon after, accompanied by him, I went to the India House, and after same formalities and the production of requisite certificates of sound health and character, I was ushered into the presence of the august Court of East India Directors, and the oath of allegiance to the Honourable East India Company was duly administered to me with other cadets. The chairman then gave us a brief address, strongly urging the importance and obvious necessity of studying the Oriental languages, without which we could not obtain preferment or be of any use; he also recommended us to treat the natives with kindness and consideration. Then, with a bow on our part, our interview ended. I subsequently paid my respects to the East India Director to whom I was indebted for my nomination, and expressed my warm thanks and obligations to him, and my earnest hope that I would do credit to my friends and himself, to which he very kindly responded and wished me all success. I subsequently received an official intimation that I had been appointed an Ensign in the Honourable East India Company's service on the Bombay Establishment. This was at my request, as I had relatives there. I was also granted extra leave of one month, to proceed *viâ* the Continent, where my family resided. A few more days were spent in town, obtaining my outfit and regimentals, and saying farewell to friends. At length, about the middle of December, leaving the Golden Cross Hotel in company with a clerical relative, I bade adieu to old England, and, crossing the Channel, duly arrived at Paris. My few days in this lively and gay city were spent in visiting the principal objects of interest, such as the Louvre, Cathedral of Notre Dame, Invalides, etc. Here I bade a last adieu to the best of uncles; for, alas! I never saw him again, but I shall ever love and revere his memory for his great kindness and generosity to me and mine.

Leaving Paris by diligence, I proceeded to Lyons, and thence to Marseilles, and dined on Christmas Day with the

British Consul, to whom I had a letter of introduction. The following day I proceeded by steamer to Genoa, and during the few hours of our stay there a friend took me a charming drive overlooking the town, whence we had a glorious view of the fine Bay of Genoa, *La Superba*. Resuming our voyage, we arrived the following day at Leghorn, where I was affectionately greeted by my dear parents and family, whom I had not seen for some years, and was also warmly welcomed by old friends who had known me in early boyhood.

It was a source of delight to me to renew my acquaintance with *La bella Italia,* for which I have ever retained a warm affection. I revisited old haunts, the beautiful promenade and drive of L'Ardenza along the seashore recalling the happy associations and sweet memories connected with our pleasant villa near Monte Nero, the abode of our childhood. How charming it was of an evening, even at this season, to sit on some quiet spot on the hillside, dotted here and there with elegant villas gleaming out from among the richest and most beautiful of shores, and gaze with enraptured eye on the ever-varying landscape of *La campagna felice,* and on the glorious expanse of the blue tide-less sea that lay at our feet!

Besides these pleasant recreations, my time was pretty well occupied with lessons in riding, dancing, as well as drilling by an Italian sergeant, and social duties.

But, alas! too swiftly passed away my happy brief month's leave, for early in February I bade farewell once more, and for an indefinite period, to the parental roof and its dear inmates. I cast many long, lingering looks behind as we steamed out of the roads, feeling, as many others have felt under similar circumstances, unspeakably wretched and lonely. I struggled, however, against giving way to despondency, and by degrees recovered my spirits as we duly arrived at Naples.

I was indeed charmed with this my first view of the fine and picturesque city, with its glorious surroundings and magnificent bay dotted with islands, and Mount Vesuvius towering above it, altogether forming a *coup d'oeil* perhaps unsurpassed in the world, and making one somewhat indulgent to the proud boast of its inhabitants: *Vedi Napoli e poi mori* (See Naples and then die!).

Leaving the far-famed city about noon, we passed through the Straits of Messina, the supposed dreaded *Scylla and Charybdis* of the ancients, and arrived at Malta on the 8th, where I was hospitably entertained by a friend of my family, till the arrival of the P. & O. steamer for Alexandria. During the interval I visited the celebrated cathedral with its altar-gates of solid silver, the fine harbour and fortifications, and the little creek where St. Paul landed when he was shipwrecked, now called *St. Paul's Bay*.

On the arrival of the mail steamer I went on board, and found three other cadets, with whom I soon fraternised, and also a gentleman, Mr. S., a partner of one of the leading mercantile firms of Bombay, who introduced himself to me, having been asked by mutual friends to interest himself in my welfare, and he subsequently proved a staunch friend.

Under his wing I landed at Alexandria amid a babel of yelling and squabbling Egyptian porters. We visited the celebrated obelisk Pompey's Pillar, covered with hieroglyphics of cuneiform character, and also that wonderful relic of antiquity Cleopatra's Needle, presented by the Khedive to the British Government, which was lying prostrate on the seashore, and which now, through the patriotic generosity of the late Sir Erasmus Wilson, adorns the Thames embankment. We subsequently proceeded by canal boat on the Nile to grand Cairo, and mounted on active little donkeys visited the great bazaar and city with its wonderful Oriental sights, which reminded one forcibly of the *Arabian Nights*; thence to the citadel, whence we obtained a fine view of the great, mysterious pyramids, and of the surrounding country.

Soon after we started to cross the desert to Suez in covered vans, drawn by vicious, ill-trained horses, which gave us much trouble, frequently lying down, and forcing the gentlemen to get out and put their shoulders to the wheel. On arrival at the mid-station we halted for refreshments, and to meet and exchange news with the homeward Indian passengers who had arrived there.

Here a singularly romantic incident befell me, which was destined to exercise an important influence over my life, for among the passengers from India was Mr. W., the partner of my friend who introduced me to him. He had his daughter, a fair-haired girlie, sitting on his knee, and this little lady some eighteen years after became my wife! Truly an *oasis* in the desert!

On reaching Suez we at once went on board the Hon. Co.'s steamer *Berenice,* and steamed rapidly down the Red Sea, catching a distant view of Mount Sinai. My friend, who was well versed in biblical history, pointed out to me the site where, according to the best authorities and tradition, the stupendous miracle in favour of God's chosen people was enacted, when "the Red Sea was divided into two parts." I believe the place is called by the natives *Mousa Ayin,* or Wells of Moses. Passing through the Straits of Babelmandeb, we duly reached Aden— the first military station or outpost in this part of the world of our vast Indian Empire, and from its important strategic position styled the *Gibraltar of the East.* It is, however, a most uninviting-looking place, being merely composed of high, barren rocks, apparently of volcanic origin. Some officers came on board, and I was struck by their being dressed entirely in white, with solar helmets, a cool and comfortable dress, which with their bronzed appearance was very becoming.

On landing I proceeded with a party riding on donkeys to visit the celebrated ancient Turkish tanks in the *Crater Camp,* some four miles off, and here I got my first glimpse of the *sipahees,* or native soldiers of our Indian Army, who looked soldier-like. How little did I dream that some twenty years after I should hold command of this very camp with all its sad

15

memories! Quitting this dreary place, we resumed our voyage, and about sunset arrived at Bombay on the 13th March 1844. Soon after a letter was brought to me with an invitation from some old friends of my family to stay with them, and saying a carriage awaited me on the *apollo bundur*, or landing-place. This kind offer I gladly accepted, and was driven through a motley crowd of dusky natives to their charming villa or bungalow covered with flowering creepers on Malabar Hill, and was warmly welcomed by them.

My first night on shore was by no means a pleasant one, for what with the torments of mosquitoes (in spite of mosquito nets), the strange surroundings, and the dismal cry of jackals, I got little sleep. However, a refreshing bath and good breakfast soon set me right. In the morning I was much struck with the splendid view from the bungalow, having on one side the fine bay, dotted with numerous vessels and skiffs, with its islands, the city, and Colaba Lighthouse at the extreme point, and on the other side the glorious expanse of the Indian Ocean, with its truly refreshing breezes.

The day after my arrival I reported myself to the Adjutant-General, to whom I had a letter of introduction, and was granted a month's leave with the option of being attached to a regiment at the gay and large station of Poona, or a native regiment at the quiet little station of Sattara. He recommended the latter, which of course I gladly accepted, and my name duly appeared in General Orders to that effect.

And now commenced my career of life in earnest as an officer, with all its responsibilities.

At the close of this my first day spent on Indian soil I made sundry good resolutions, and indulged it may be in some rather heroic dreams, but at all events the result was not altogether un-practical, for I resolved to make at least a good start by at once setting to work to study the Oriental, languages.

CHAPTER 2

First Experiences of India

Bombay, the seat of the Western Presidency and the commercial emporium of India, could at this time boast of little
architectural beauty, the only public buildings deserving of
any notice being the Cathedral, the Town Hall, Elphinstone
College, and the Jamsetjee Jeejeebhoy Hospital.

It is, however, a cosmopolitan city, presenting a greater variety of picturesque groups and scenes than perhaps any other
city, not excepting Cairo. I used greatly to enjoy a drive in
the evening through the densely populated native town and
Bendy Bazaar, a living panorama, so novel and full of interest
to my unaccustomed eyes. Here might be seen congregated
together people of all nations, kindreds, tribes, and languages,
from all parts of the globe: stout, hook-nosed Parsees, with
their peculiar characteristic head-dress; mild Hindoos, of various shades and denominations, in flowing robes and turbans
of varied shape and colour indicative of their respective castes;
bearded Mussulmans swaggering along with supercilious air
and gait; scowling, fierce-looking Arabs, with gaudy silk head-
dresses, surmounted by a camel-hair turban, and enveloped in
the striped camel-hair cloak ; fair Persians with embroidered
vests and tall, conical lamb-skin caps ; powerful-looking *Seed-
ees* or Africans with their coal-black skins and thick blubber
lips; Chinese with their long pigtails, high cheek-bones, and
queer-looking eyes; sleepy-looking Turks in their *tarboosh* or

red fez caps; fair-skinned Armenians; swarthy Jews; Portuguese padres in long black gowns; sunburnt British tars driving furiously along in hack buggies, or rolling about the streets; policemen, armed with staves, in their blue tunics and yellow turbans: these and many other tribes—Malays, Indians, Egyptians, Abyssinians, etc.—formed altogether a scene hardly to be equalled anywhere.

Then there were the endless processions : now a bridal party, anon a funeral accompanied by torch-bearers, and a crowd creating a fearful hubbub, increased by the clang of discordant instruments,— tom-toms, etc.,—so that one may form some idea of this Oriental scene.

Emerging from this hideous babel and stifling atmosphere on to the esplanade, the Prado, or drive by the seashore, how truly refreshing and reviving was the sea-breeze, after a steaming, sultry day!

Around the band-stand, the general rendezvous and centre of attraction, whence issued strains of operatic or martial music, would be congregated the elite and fashion of Bombay—some in carriages, others riding or walking on the green sward; officers in gay uniforms, mounted on spirited Arabs, paying their devoirs to the ladies; and troops of children attended by their copper-coloured ayahs—all these helped to give life and animation to the brilliant scene. To my taste, however, the most enjoyable time on these occasions was after sunset, when the moon had risen, and, the music stealing into your ears, you inhaled the sea-breeze and indulged in a *tête-à-tête* with some fair companion; or, if in a contemplative mood, you reclined in your carriage, and gave yourself up to pleasing reveries of home and absent friends.

Strolling along the seashore, it was a curious and striking sight to watch the Parsees (fire-worshippers) at their devotions, with eyes fixed on the setting sun and prostrating themselves to the earth, in which position they remained some time, repeating their prayers aloud, and thus reminding one strongly of the Pharisees of old. Mussulmans may also be seen at this time kneeling on their little praying carpets, with faces turned towards Mecca, mumbling their prayers and counting their beads. I noticed also several fires close to the seaside, and was informed that these were the bodies of Hindoos being cremated, their ashes being thrown into the sea. These and similar sights cannot fail to attract the attention of everyone, and more especially a new arrival. It has often struck me that one great advantage of visiting the East is, that it enables one more fully to understand and appreciate the manners and customs, as well as the illustrations from Eastern life, which are to be met with in the Holy Scriptures.

Among the lions of Bombay are the celebrated Buddhist Caves of Elephanta, situated on the island of that name, and so called from a colossal figure of that animal cut out of the solid rock and near the landing-place. It is a favourite place for pic-nic excursions, and in company with some friends I crossed the harbour in a bunder boat, and visited these very curious rock temples, which from their great antiquity are well worth seeing. They are divided into three compartments supported by massive pillars, on which are carved huge, hideous-look-ing figures of various heathen gods in very good preservation considering the many centuries which have elapsed since they were first cut. The island itself is a dense jungle, and by no means a desirable abode, being considered unhealthy. It was formerly the resort of snakes and other unpleasant animals.

Having, with the assistance of my friend's native butler, completed my arrangements, and obtained a staff of the requi-site number of servants, and secured also a tent, I took leave of my kind hosts, and left Bombay at the end of March for Sattara *viâ* Nagotna to join the 2nd Grenadiers, to which   regiment I was attached to do duty till posted or gazetted to some corps, which would not be for some months. I embarked in a bunder boat, and reached Nagotna on the evening of the same day, thence driving by phaeton through a jungle or forest to the village of Mhar. Resuming my journey, I enjoyed a delightful moonlight drive to the foot of the ghauts, notwithstanding being nearly upset by the furious driving of my *jehu*. Here I found a *palkee* or palanquin with twelve bearers awaiting me in which to perform the ascent; but this mode of travelling uphill proved so awkward and uncomfortable that I preferred walking up the greater part of the way, and was rewarded by witnessing what seemed to me a very striking scene. In front were men carrying huge flaming torches followed by my *palkee* borne by several swarthy, half-naked bearers, uttering a monotonous chant as they laboured up the steep ascent, each holding in his hand by way of support a long bamboo stick somewhat resembling an alpenstock; then came my servants with the baggage, the rear being brought up by more torch-bearers. It was about midnight, and as the procession wound slowly up the steep mountain path, by dark, overhanging precipices, and along the edge of deep, tigerish-looking ravines clothed in a thick jungle, the torches throwing a lurid glare around and on the dusky forms of the *hamauls* (or bearers), the effect was weird and somewhat funereal, reminding me strongly of some similar theatrical scene I had witnessed.

Arriving at the summit of the Mahabuleshwur Hills, a favourite resort and sanatorium of the Bombay Presidency during the hot weather, several thousand feet above the sea-level, I remained there three days, and was so charmed with it and the magnificent scenery around, that I resolved as soon as I could get leave to revisit it.

Early on the morning of 4th April I descended the ghauts on pony-back, and here I saw for the first time in my life that remarkable phenomenon the *mirage*, the valley below appearing to me as a miniature lake; for at first I certainly mistook what I saw to be a sheet of water! On reaching a traveller's bungalow, where I slept, I strolled into an adjoining village, and observed a Hindoo temple in which was enshrined a hideous idol, like a monkey, painted in bright vermilion; this was their god, which the poor benighted creatures washed daily (being summoned to the operation by sound of a trumpet), and to which they paid their devotions and made propitiatory offerings of rice, fruit, etc.

There was also a kind of altar in the neighbourhood of this temple made of large rough stones placed upright in a circle, with one much larger than the rest daubed with red paint, in the centre of which they worshipped, reminding one of the Druids of old—a melancholy sight!

The next day I arrived at Sattara, the end of my journey, and reporting myself to the adjutant of the regiment, was introduced by him to Colonel H., the commanding officer, who received me most kindly, and invited me to stay with him for a few days, which invitation I gladly accepted. The Colonel afterwards took me to the mess and introduced me to the officers, who were a gentlemanly set, among them being two unposted ensigns who had passed the India House on the same day as I did. The Colonel and his daughter were extremely kind, and he, with great consideration, arranged for me to *chum* with one of the nicest subalterns; and thus commenced my first experience of housekeeping on my own account.

The daily life at Sattara, as at most Indian stations, after the novelty has worn off, is certainly dull and monotonous, the arrival of the regular overland mail with our European letters being the greatest event of the month; and we poor exiles fully realised the truth of Solomon's words, "As cold water to a thirsty soul, so is good news from a far country."

Soon after my arrival I was ordered by the adjutant to attend drill till further orders, and was duly initiated into the mysteries of the *goose-step*, etc., in company with two other *Griffs*, or new arrivals.

I had scarcely settled down here when I received the sad news of the death of a cousin of mine of about my own age, whom I had looked forward to meeting soon; he died at Deesa, and belonged to a distinguished regiment, and was much liked.

Having made considerable progress in our military duties, we young unattached officers were permitted to go to the Mahabuleshwur Hills for a few days' leave, the heat being oppressive. On arrival we pitched our tent in an open space not far from a ravine, a very picturesque spot, but not altogether conducive to our comfort, as we were much disturbed at night by the cries of hyenas, jackals, and other animals prowling about in our neighbourhood.

Having purchased a strong Deccan *tattoo*, or pony, I enjoyed many delightful rides among the lovely sylvan and English park-like roads, shadowed by fine trees with low, overhanging branches. The latter, however, were very dangerous to horsemen, one or two fatal accidents having occurred here. I also had thereby a somewhat narrow escape on one occasion, as my pony, which proved vicious and hard-mouthed, took it into his head to run away with me, so that my position was anything but enviable, being within a yard of a precipice some three thousand feet deep, and in danger of having my head dashed against some of these low-hanging branches! However, I managed eventually to pull him up.

It is truly a glorious and impressive sight to witness a tropical thunderstorm, the first burst of the monsoon or rainy season among these noble mountains. The brows of the hills are wrapped in a sullen mist, while dark, rolling masses of clouds come down over the mountains; floods of rain pour in raging torrents down the steep and rocky sides, forming splendid waterfalls; while startling flashes of dazzling lightning light up with a lurid glare the dark valley beneath; this is quickly followed by intense darkness, and terrific bursts of thunder echoing afar among the distant hills; then comes the delicious calm, when all nature, which lately seemed so fearfully agitated, appears once more soft and smiling. How reviving is the sensation! how great the sense of relief which this contrast affords, succeeded as it usually is by a beautifully clear evening and glorious sunset, the sea, dotted with little specks of ships, being often visible, while the sun like a ball of fire sinks slowly below the horizon, bathing it in a golden flood of glory!

To the sportsman also this health resort of the Bombay Presidency offers great attractions, as the dense jungles around and below in the Koinar valley are the resort of tigers, panthers, bears, and other denizens of the forest.

Having thoroughly enjoyed our brief sojourn, and our leave having expired, we returned to camp in time for *muster parade*. Immediately afterwards, having engaged a good *moonshee*, or teacher, I attacked the Hindustani language in good earnest, being determined to pass my examination at Bombay as soon as possible.

In September I attended for the first time the *durbar*, or levée, of a native prince, His Highness the Rajah of Sattara, which, although a somewhat stupid, formal affair, was interesting to me from its novelty. All the officers were in full-dress uniforms, and the Resident (Colonel Ovans) formally presented us individually to His Highness, who shook hands with each in turn. On being seated, *nautch-girls* gorgeously bedecked with jewels and bedizened with gold and brocade, wearing large nose and ear rings and small silver anklets with bells attached to their feet, sang doleful love-ditties in a monotonous tone, to an accompaniment of native music, while they swayed their flexible bodies into various voluptuous attitudes. During the intervals fragrant otto of roses was sprinkled over us, and on the termination of the ceremony a wreath of *mogree*, or jessamine, was thrown over the neck of each of us.

The wives of the Rajah and their attendants, I was told, could see all that was going on without themselves being visible.

This quiet little station or cantonment has a picturesque appearance, and during the monsoon, as it is cool and pleasant, it is enlivened by a few visitors. The most agreeable drive is the *Sangum-Maolce*, where the sacred rivers the Krishna and the Yemna join. A row of magnificent banyan trees, so closely planted and their branches interlaced as almost to have the

23

appearance of one tree, lines the road on either side, forming a broad avenue of about two miles to the junction of the rivers. On both banks are elaborately carved Hindoo stone temples and handsome tombs where troops of monkeys disport themselves with impunity, being held sacred by the natives. It is melancholy to think that at this place many a horrid *suttee* has been perpetrated, not only in days of old, but even in comparatively recent times, and many a poor widow has been forced to ascend the funeral pile while her shrieks were drowned by the barbarous tom-toms and the shouts of the insane multitude.

Soon after this period alarming tidings reached us that a portion of the Southern Mahratta country had broken out into insurrection, and that the political officer who had been sent by Government to inquire into the matter had been taken prisoner into the strong fort of Punàla. The Government at once took energetic steps to punish these audacious rebels, and a field force was speedily organised to proceed to the disturbed district, of which the regiment to which I was attached was to form a part. This caused great excitement amongst us. Not wishing to be left behind (though only attached to and not belonging to the regiment), I applied to go, a request which the Colonel at first did not grant; but, through the kind mediation of the Major, I was eventually allowed to go as a *volunteer*, to my great delight, as I was anxious to see a little active service, which would be a novel experience for an ensign as yet *un-posted* to a regiment.

There were, however, two drawbacks to this: one being that my study of the language would be interrupted, and I should be unable to pass the Presidency examination within the year as I had hoped; and the other was that I found, owing to being a *volunteer*, I would not be entitled to the extra allowance granted to officers for carriage of tent, baggage, etc., which was a rather serious pecuniary matter to me.

CHAPTER 3

Southern Mahratta Campaign

The troops, European and native, which left Sattara early in October 1844 formed a compact little force of infantry and irregular cavalry with two guns and a hundred sappers. And now began my initiation into Indian campaigning, which, when the novelty wore off, was tiresome enough, what with the night marches, when we plodded slowly along, perhaps losing our way crossing nullahs swollen by the rains, which still continued; the fatigue of being many hours in the saddle; and the anything but pleasing rear-guard duty of bringing up the baggage and stragglers, exposed to a scorching sun. Then, on entering the disturbed districts, came outlying and inlying pickets and false alarms; one of these, I remember, being caused by our little doctor nervously discharging his pistol in the middle of the night (for which he was sharply reprimanded), and other disagreeable incidents connected with a march through an enemy's country. After recrossing the river Krishna we arrived at Kolapore about the 28th October, and encamped under a grove of trees near some Hindoo temples. Shortly after I had the pleasure of dining with one of the Madras native regiments, commanded by Colonel Wallace, who during this campaign distinguished himself, while in pursuit of the insurgents, by performing an extraordinary feat, which earned for him the sobriquet of the *Hero of the Elephant Rock*. This was a scarped precipice the descent of which he with his men, guns, and baggage accomplished by means of ropes, without any accident, in the immediate vicinity of the enemy, whom he defeated.

Here also I met for the first time a still more distinguished officer, Colonel, afterwards Sir James, Outram, G.C.B., *the Bayard of the Indian Army* (as Sir Charles Napier styled him), who was acting as our Political Officer, and under whom I had subsequently the honour to serve in Persia.

The field force which was here assembled under the command of General de la Motte, C.B., numbered altogether about ten thousand of all ranks. It was composed of European and native troops drawn from the Presidencies of Madras and Bombay, and was divided into three brigades, the one to which I was attached being commanded by our Colonel. Scarcely had we reached Kolapore and joined the field force when orders were issued for two companies of our regiment, under Captain Clarke, to go in pursuit of some rebels in the district; but when our enemies heard of our approach they thought prudence the better part of valour, and hastily decamped, and we were soon recalled.

Our troops took military possession of the town, and guards were posted night and day at all the gates with stringent orders to allow of no egress or ingress without a *pass* from the political agent, as it was strongly suspected that the Rajah, or native ruler, and his people were both aiding and in active communication with the insurgents.

The town of Kolapore, the capital of the State of that name, is rather a fine one, with its palace and square, and is entered by a lofty and handsomely carved stone gateway with side arches, not unlike that at the Horse Guards, though on a smaller scale. It stands in a valley embraced on three sides by a range of hills on which to the north-west are situated, adjoining each other, the hill fortresses of Punàla and Pownghur, which are deemed impregnable by the natives, being perched on rocks some three hundred feet high, with natural ramparts presenting perpendicular scarps of some forty or fifty feet all round. On the bastions were mounted several guns and jingals, or wall-pieces, in the use of which the enemy proved themselves expert. Here the rebels had entrenched themselves, and unfurled the standard of revolt, bidding us defiance.

The position of poor Colonel Ovans, who had been treacherously taken prisoner and confined in the larger fort of Punàla, was certainly a critical one, but it was sternly intimated to the rebels that if any injury were done to this high representative of the Government, a terrible retribution would be exacted from them. It was also determined by the General to act with promptitude and attack the forts at once. Accordingly, the *pettah*, or suburbs, being cleared in gallant style by the brigade to which I belonged, breaching batteries were speedily erected, and troops having been posted around and in the gorge of the ravine between the two forts to cut off the escape of fugitives, the gates were burst open, and the storming party, surmounting all obstacles by their bravery and enthusiasm, gallantly rushed up the breach, forced an entrance, not without some difficulty, and caused much loss to the enemy, several of whom were killed when attempting to escape, and among them their chief. On the capture of Punàla, Pownghur surrendered. Our casualties were comparatively small, but we had to deplore the loss of our worthy Commander, Colonel Hickes, who was killed by a round shot. He was much esteemed and deservedly regretted, especially by his own regiment, few having greater cause to do so than myself.

On entering the fort, it was a great relief to find that Colonel Ovans was safe, though he had had a narrow escape, not only from the hands of the enemy, but also from one of our own shells, which fell near him. While, however, rejoicing at his own happy escape, he was not a little affected at learning the fate of the rebel chief, by whom he had been well treated and to whose firmness he was mainly indebted for his life.

After the capture of the forts I, in company with another

officer, visited the larger one—Punàla; and it was a source of wonder to us how the storming party ever managed to climb up so steep and apparently inaccessible a path under fire ; and we both felt that nothing but British pluck and the strong excitement of the moment could have achieved such success. In fact, Colonel Peat, who acted as chief engineer, declared it was a smarter affair than *Guznee*, of which we heard so much in England and at the capture of which he had been present.

By way of souvenirs, I procured sundry trophies, including a long two-handed Mahratta sword— something like a Scotch claymore—and some curious well-carved stone figures of Hindoo gods, etc. When exploring this captured fort how little did I dream that, many years after, my daughter and little grandson would be quietly residing there (it having been converted into a hill sanatorium), and that my son-in-law would hold an important position in connection with His Highness the Maharajah of Kolapore! Verily truth is often stranger than fiction!

Soon after this that fearful Asiatic scourge, the cholera, made its appearance among the troops encamped in the neighbourhood; but, fortunately, it was not of a virulent type, and after we had changed our ground it gradually disappeared.

Early in December I was gazetted to the Bombay Rifles, and I was warmly congratulated by my friends on being appointed to so distinguished a regiment which had served at the great siege and capture of Seringapatam under the Duke of Wellington (then Sir A. Wellesley), and is now called *The Wellesley Rifles* in honour of the great Duke. It was also the only regular rifle regiment of the Indian Army with its full complement of European and native officers. It bears among its many appointments the word "Bourbon" *(Ile de France),* the regiment having been present at the capture of that island from the French and crossed bayonets with them.

Shortly after my appointment I received an offer to exchange into a distinguished European regiment, and, on consulting my friends and senior officers, was advised not to do so, on the grounds that as there were double the number of officers in a European regiment the promotion was slower and the expenses greater, while there would be fewer facilities and opportunities of studying Oriental languages, which I was anxious to do; so I declined, and never had reason to regret this refusal.

As there appeared little prospect of further active service, other forts having been captured or surrendered, I obtained leave to join my regiment, which was stationed at Baroda in Guzerat. Accordingly, taking advantage of a detachment returning to Sattara, I accompanied them, and duly reached that place, where I spent my first Christmas in India, dining at the hospitable mess of the 6th Regiment Native Infantry. My stay here, however, was a very brief one, for on New Year's Eve I left for Bombay, *viâ* the ghauts, having obtained a month's leave, in order to procure there some of my new rifle equipments (though I had to obtain my full dress from home), and on arrival was warmly greeted by my kind friends there.

On the expiry of my leave I took my departure for Cambay in a *pattimar*, or country coasting vessel—a distance of some two hundred and fifty miles. This boat was of primitive shape and rude construction, and it was filled with heterogeneous articles besides my own household goods, servants, horse, goat, poultry, etc.—in fact, somewhat in the Noah's-Ark style. As we coasted along I was much struck with the view of the Western Ghauts, —"the backbone of India," as they are called,—a lofty range of mountains presenting a very bold and picturesque outline. After hugging the shore, and tumbling about the Gulf of Cambay for some clays, and nearly running short of provisions, we reached Cambay, an ancient town formerly of great note, but now much dilapidated. The Cambay stones, agates, cornelians, etc., found here are celebrated, being beautifully polished and wrought into a variety of ornaments.

On landing I proceeded northwards by bullock-cart to Kaira, about forty miles off, to pay a visit to a kind relative who then commanded there. This was formerly a large station for European troops, but, proving very unhealthy owing to the malaria rising from the clamp and marshy soil, it was subsequently abandoned. Not far from the banks of the river is a Protestant church, in the churchyard of which an extraordinary scene occurred shortly before my arrival. A funeral was the occasion, and my relative, in the absence of a chaplain, was reading the burial service beside the open grave, when the party was suddenly attacked by a swarm of angry wasps which their presence had disturbed. Manfully did they hold their ground for some time, but at length human nature could stand it no longer, and hastily finishing the service, they all fled, and jumped into the river to escape from their tormentors!

Having taken leave of my relatives, from whom I received good advice, I started for my final destination, Baroda, being provided with an escort in consequence of the many thieves in that neighbourhood, and reached Baroda early in March 1845. On my arrival I at once called on the adjutant to report myself, and in the evening joined my brother officers at mess.

The cantonment of Baroda is rather a picturesque and striking one, with its fine parade ground, admirably adapted for parade purposes, being an open undulating plain clothed with noble trees, giving it a park-like appearance. This was the usual rendezvous, where the regimental band played twice a week in the evening to enliven us a little. The most prominent object in the neighbourhood of camp is the Residency, a handsome, massive-looking building with extensive gardens, and having much the appearance of an English hall slightly orientalised, and where Sir R. Arbuthnot was Resident.

As soon as I got comfortably settled in a small bungalow I secured the services of an intelligent *moonshee*, and again resumed in earnest my study of Hindustani, which had been interrupted. On one occasion I attended the durbar of this native prince, and from a balcony witnessed a fight between an elephant and a rhinoceros, got up specially for our amusement, in which the latter proved victorious.

Occasionally we had picnic excursions and some deer-shooting, or were invited by His Highness to witness deer-stalking with his trained cheetahs or hunting leopards. It was a curious and wonderful sight to watch their stealthy, cat-like motions as they caught sight of their game, taking advantage of every cover, tree, bush, or stone, with glaring eyes fixed on their prey, and then suddenly swooping down on it with tremendous bounds.

Some months later an interesting ceremony took place, viz., the decoration with the Order of British India of our old and worthy Subahdar-Major as a reward of upwards of forty years' distinguished service, he having been present at the siege of Seringapatam under Sir A. Wellesley. He was of Jewish extraction, by name Suliman-Israel, but of a very different type and disposition to that attributed to his brethren; for he insisted, as he was about to retire on his well-earned pension, on giving a champagne dinner to the officers; a gala performance in the shape of a grand *nautch* to the native officers and men; and fireworks, etc., for the station generally. To invest him with this order of merit with due dignity, a brigade parade was assembled, the troops being in full dress, and the handsome decoration was pinned on his breast, and the brigadier made a little speech. At our mess after dinner the native officers came in, dressed in their handsome, becoming native costumes, and being seated, the President proposed the health of the venerable and excellent Subahdar-Major in a neat Hindustani speech, expressing the general regret at his departure, and hoping he would long enjoy his pension. The Subahdar-Major then rose and returned thanks very gracefully, and seemed much affected at bidding farewell to the old regiment in which he had been brought up from childhood.

In October the Hindoo festival of the *Dussera* was celebrated with great pomp, when H.H., seated in state on an elephant and accompanied by a huge crowd, proceeded to a temple, and cast into the river some painted heathen gods. A guard of honour in command of a European officer used to be present, but I am thankful to say this countenancing of an idolatrous Hindoo festival has been discontinued.

The climate of Baroda is very trying, especially just after the monsoon, when it is very hot and muggy, while insects of every description, as well as snakes, cause extreme annoyance. One of these horrid reptiles on one occasion at mess crawled up the back of an officer's chair, and with head reared and expanded hood was in close proximity to his unconscious victim, when a brother officer seated by, with great presence of mind, by a sudden back-hander threw it off and killed it, thus probably saving his friend's life; for it proved to be a deadly cobra!

Having made considerable progress in Hindustani and passed the usual examination before the Station Committee, I proceeded to Bombay about the beginning of December to appear before the presidency examiners; and having secured the services of one of the best teachers, received the strongest encouragement as to passing the great examination in January. But here again my plans were upset, for no sooner had I settled down in a tent on the esplanade than I learnt, to my great surprise, that my regiment was *en route* to Bombay, being under orders to proceed to Scinde on field service!

The regiment soon after arrived at Bombay, and was duly inspected by the Commander-in-Chief. I of course had to re-join it as it was going on service, and to put off the presidency examination, contenting myself with passing the colloquial one, without which I was not qualified to hold charge of a company.

CHAPTER 4

Field Service in Scinde

Our regiment, soon after its inspection by the Commander-in-Chief, embarked for Scinde, under command of Lieutenant-Colonel Forbes, on board a transport, and after a pleasant sail of ten days reached the port of Kurrachee.

On landing we were marching to the cantonment, about three miles off, when we were met by a remarkable-looking personage of singularly Jewish physiognomy, with long white beard, wearing a plain surtout and white solar helmet. He was alone, and galloping up to us, in a voice of authority he ordered us to halt and wheel into line, when he rode up and down the ranks, minutely inspecting us with his piercing eyes. This was none other than General Sir Charles Napier, the *hero of Meanee* and conqueror of Scinde, who was also Governor and Commander-in-Chief of the province, and who was styled by the natives *Shaitan-Ke-bhaee*, or the devil's brother!

This very gruesome title was doubtless owing, not only to his determined character as a successful general, but also to the feeling of many that his treatment of the Ameers—the former rulers of the country—had been unjust and harsh, which opinion was shared by Colonel Outram, the Political Agent, who gave a practical proof of his sincerity by declining to touch his handsome share of prize money, and handing it over to a charitable society in Bombay. *Punch* also humorously suggested that *Peccavi* (I have sinned) would have been an appropriate despatch by Sir Charles on the occasion!

The seaport of Kurrachee—the *Alexandria of the Indus*—is from its geographical position a place of great importance, for it not only commands the Indus, but is also the outlet of Central Asia. The harbour is somewhat difficult of approach, and at its entrance is the fort of Minora on a rocky headland.

About this period (1846) momentous and stirring events, big with the fate of nations and the future of India, were being enacted on the banks of the Sutlej. Two desperate and doubtful battles had been fought by us with the Sikhs, by far the most warlike, the bravest, and most disciplined troops (trained as they had been by French, Italian, and other officers) in the East, and who now dared to dispute with us for the sceptre of Hindustan! Such was the critical state of affairs when shortly after our arrival we received orders to proceed without delay by forced marches to Upper Scinde, to join the Reserve Army of the Indus forming there under the renowned General, Sir Charles Napier, G.C.B. Accordingly, passing through Ghara and Tatta, we arrived at Hyderabad, the capital of Scinde. We were much impressed by our first sight of the far-famed classic river Indus, the western boundary of India, whose source is in the heart of the snow-capped Himalayas, and which in its majestic course flows upwards of one thousand six hundred miles! Gazing on this vast expanse of water, our minds reverted to the wonderful enterprise of Alexander the Great, who, some two thousand two hundred years before, crossed this mighty stream with his Macedonian Army.

Resuming our march to Jurruck, a curious incident occurred *en route,* for a fine *sounder* or herd of wild hogs dashed through our column; and our Colonel, who was a keen sportsman, unable to resist the temptation, dashed after them, and with a spear which his groom carried killed one of them, which proved a great acquisition to our mess table. Continuing our march parallel to the river, we reached Kotree,—a naval depôt of the Indus Flotilla,—and crossing in boats arrived at Hyderabad, on the left bank of the river, where we halted for a few days.

Hyderabad, the capital of Scinde, is a large and dirty town, presenting to the eye a confused mass of mud houses, flat roofs, trees, etc., enclosed by high walls and a strong fortress, having lofty bastions and a moat, and also a massive round tower where the Ameers lived. The Residency, where Colonel Outram resided, was attacked during the war, and gallantly and successfully defended by a company of H.M.'s 22nd Regiment.

Early in January 1846 I was promoted to be a First Lieutenant, and having, as previously mentioned, passed the *colloquial examination,* got the charge of a company, which was very gratifying, and a welcome addition to my pay. Leaving Hyderabad, the regiment marched along the left bank of the river to Roree, passing by the battlefield of Meanee, where Sir Charles Napier's victory had decided the fate of the province of Scinde and annexed it to the British territories.

When *en route* we learnt that two other and more decisive battles—those of Aliwal and Sobraon—had been fought with the Sikhs, resulting in their being driven back headlong in disastrous defeat across the Sutlej, and on arrival at Roree, the headquarters of the army of the Indus, we found this great news confirmed.

After this happy termination of the first Punjáb War of 1845-46 the force was broken up and ordered into cantonments, my regiment being sent to Shikarpore.

Roree is situated close to the banks of the river, some of the houses being very lofty and overhanging it, but the streets are narrow and filthy; midway in the stream, which is here about half a mile wide, is the island fortress of Bukkur (used as an arsenal). It is now spanned by a fine railway bridge to Sukkur on the opposite side of the river, which in those early days my regiment had crossed in large flat-bottomed boats.

Sukkur, on the right bank, is a military cantonment, and, from the high limestone rocks on which it is built, has a striking appearance, with its noble river, and its banks clothed with luxuriant groves of date-palms, and its picturesque island fortress; but, alas! it is one of the most deadly climates in the East, and one of the hottest stations in India. It was here that that fine regiment, H.M.'s 78th Highlanders, some years ago suffered fearfully from fever and cholera, and it has been justly called "The Graveyard of Europeans."

I was much struck with the ingenious and curious method of catching fish here by the fishermen. They use a large oblong earthen jar, partly filled with water to steady it, and having an aperture of nine inches diameter, on which opening the fisherman places the pit of his stomach; and in this position, looking like a frog, using his feet as propellers, he captures the pulla, a delicious species of carp, with a hand-net, and deposits them in the jar! This strange method of locomotion is also adopted by natives of both sexes in crossing the river, who by its aid boldly brave the rapid and turbid stream.

From Sukkur we marched to Shikarpore, about thirty-six miles off, and relieved a Bengal regiment there about the beginning of March 1846, just as the hot weather began to set in. The appearance of this cantonment certainly did not look very inviting, being situated- in the midst of a sandy plain, while the officers' houses—being merely of plastered mud, whitewashed, with flat roofs and no gardens—had a gloomy aspect. Finding it cheaper to buy one of these mud edifices than to pay the exorbitant rents demanded, a brother officer and I bought one, and afterwards found no difficulty in disposing of it. The town is a very important one from a commercial point of view, its merchants having extensive business transactions with Central Asia, where their goods have penetrated by their *kafilas* or caravans.

The hot season lasts nearly six months, there being no monsoon in this country, the heat increasing in intensity up

to August, when it is almost unbearable, and extremely trying to the constitution. In fact, notwithstanding punkahs and
other cooling appliances, we deemed ourselves fortunate if
the thermometer was within 100°! We of course at night slept
outside (sleeping was impossible in the house) and were often
treated to dust storms, which, while somewhat cooling the
air, filled our eyes, ears, and hair with fine sand. My only relief
was to ride to a friend's house who had a swimming bath in
his garden, a dip into which was truly refreshing!

I remember my surprise on witnessing for the first time an
immense flight of locusts of great size, which literally dark-
ened the air by their countless numbers, causing more dev-
astation and ruin where they alighted than an invading army.
The lower orders of Scindians and Arabs use these insects, I
believe, as an article of food.

In this dry and thirsty land, where rain rarely falls, the ir-
rigation of the soil depends on the periodical inundations of
the river, as in Egypt, and the *Persian wheel* is much in use,
the water being carried by means of small canals in various
directions.

After vegetating some months at this station of Shikarpore,
I in the month of September proceeded in command of a
detachment of my regiment on outpost duty to Shahpore,
on the north-west frontier and bordering on Beloochistan, in
order to relieve a similar party there. Our march was indeed a
very trying one, the glare of the great plains of scorching sand
which we crossed being terrific, while the scarcity of water
was severely felt, and the sun beat down so powerfully on our
small tent that my companion and I were compelled to wrap
wet towels round our heads and get under the table, where
we lay gasping!

On arrival at Khanghur (now called Jacobabad in honour of its distinguished founder), the headquarters of the renowned Scinde Irregular Horse, the beau-ideal of irregular
cavalry, we were hospitably entertained by the officers of that

corps, including their great Commander, Major, afterwards General, Jacob, C. B.—a man of very high reputation, both as a cavalry officer, administrator, and inventor of the improved Jacob rifle which bears his name. What, however, entitles him to lasting credit is his wonderfully successful management of and mastery over the wild hill robber tribes of Beloochistan, over whom he acquired an extraordinary moral influence, by literally turning their swords into ploughshares, so that what was formerly a waste of desert is now a smiling garden!

Resuming our march, we duly reached our destination, the village of Cutch Gundava in Beloochistan, and our extreme outpost on the west within some sixty miles of the celebrated Bolan Pass. The strength of this outpost consisted of a troop of native cavalry and two companies of rifles with a gun, and their duty was to overawe and keep in check the Boogties, Murrees, and other hill robber tribes who made forages on the peaceful villages of the plains like the Caterans of old, carrying off their cattle and goods. Recently they had received a severe lesson from our troops, several of them having been cut up and the cattle and goods recovered, so they were comparatively quiet at present. The number of fierce pariah dogs in this district was enormous, causing serious annoyance, and our only excitement was in hunting them down. A sad accident, however, had recently occurred to a young cavalry officer, who while thus engaged collided violently with another rider, and being thrown from his horse, was killed on the spot.

We found provisions here very scarce, there being nothing procurable except miserable fowls and tough goat's meat. As for vegetables, we had to content ourselves mostly with onions and rice. However, we occasionally got supplies sent us from our mess on a swift camel, so that on Christmas Day we fared sumptuously!

During my solitary rides in the surrounding desert I was frequently deceived by that strange optical delusion the mirage, that mocks the eye by giving to a line of vapour in the distance the appearance of lakes, palaces, and temples, etc., which on approach vanish like "the baseless fabric of a dream." In this neighbourhood a great number of camels are reared by the Jhats, a wandering tribe. The milk of the camel is greatly esteemed by them, but to me it tasted coarse and bitter.

After remaining some months in this dreary hole we were to our great joy relieved about the beginning of 1847, and it was with a sense of great relief that we turned our backs upon it, and duly reached headquarters at Shikarpore. The regiment soon after received orders in February to proceed to Kurrachee, as Sir Charles Napier wished to have us under his own eye, and we were brigaded with the 60th Rifles—a crack rifle corps.

Leaving Shikarpore under command of Major Honner, a fine officer, we marched to Sukkur, and there embarking on steamers arrived at Tatta, where we landed and marched to Kurrachee, arriving about the end of February 1847.

A few days after we called officially in a body on General Sir Charles Napier, G.C.B., being introduced individually by our commanding officer.

Kurrachee, by contrast with Shikarpore, impressed us favourably, there being more life and gaiety, it being the headquarters of the Scinde Division of the army, which consisted of two European and two Indian regiments with horse and foot artillery, etc. It is generally considered a healthy station (though the previous year it had been visited by cholera) and has the advantage of the sea-breezes, the little village of Clifton-on-Sea, a few miles off, being the principal promenade and drive, where we occasionally enjoyed a dip and swim in the sea. It is also used as a sanatorium for European invalids. The Government Gardens is a favourite resort, where the various regimental bands play of an evening, and where there is also a fine aviary and a swimming bath.

In the month of April 1848 I obtained leave of absence to

proceed to Bombay to undergo the Presidency examination in Hindustani, and after all my disappointments I had the satisfaction of successfully passing the ordeal, and on rejoining my regiment was at once appointed Interpreter of it, and also soon after acted as such for the 1st European Fusiliers. This double duty was by no means a sinecure, as court-martials were the order of the day, three local lieutenants being tried for embezzlement of public money.

About this period (1848) our distinguished Commander, General Sir Charles Napier, was about to retire and proceed to Europe, and a farewell banquet was given to him by the station in our mess-house, which was the largest in camp. A great number were present, including many officers who had served under him; and when his health was drunk with all honours, I gazed with much interest on the aged warrior as he stood up and replied in manly and feeling terms, bidding farewell to us all.

Although my time was pretty well occupied with my regimental duties, as well as those of interpreter at court-martials, I determined to attach the Mahrattee language, an occupation which I occasionally enlivened by a boating excursion to Minora Point, or a picnic to Clifton or *Muggur Tulao* (the Alligators' Pool), about nine miles from camp. This large tank swarms with these ugly monsters, who are fed and protected by some religious mendicants, and it is an extraordinary sight to watch these voracious monsters being fed with a wretched goat. What had appeared to be a mere inanimate mass was now seen to be suddenly fighting and struggling for their prey!

The Kurrachee Races were considered very good, our Brigadier being a patron of the turf, and these with amateur theatricals helped to enliven our sojourn there.

Little rain falls here, but I remember a terrific thunderstorm, accompanied by forked lightning, which struck one of the Government buildings, setting it on fire and doing much damage. Being on duty that day, I had to remain many hours with a working-party until the fire was extinguished, the Sipahees vieing with their European comrades in their successful efforts to overcome it.

In the month of September, having made good progress in the Mahrattee language, and passed the usual preliminary Committee, which was presided over by Captain Burton, the celebrated Oriental linguist and African traveller, I proceeded to Bombay for the Presidency examination ; but to the surprise of my friends I was not successful, notwithstanding the encouragement I had received from Captain Burton and the fact that I had, since passing the Station Committee, acted as interpreter in that language. However, on rejoining the regiment, my commanding officer appointed me both quartermaster and paymaster in addition to interpreter to the regiment, and in these capacities I served throughout the second Punjáb campaign, as described in the next chapter.

Chapter 5

Second Punjab Campaign

The Siege and Storming of Mooltan

The cause and origin of the second Punjáb campaign, resulting in the annexation of the Punjáb, was a truly melancholy one. The Indian Government deputed Mr. Vans Agnew
of the Bengal Civil Service to take over charge of the fortress
of Mooltan and district from the Governor, Dewan Moolraj,
and Lieutenant Anderson of the Bombay Fusiliers (a brother-in-law of Sir James Outram) was selected as his assistant.
When taking leave of this latter amiable officer, and offering
him all good wishes at our mess (where he was my guest), little did we dream of the sad and tragic fate that awaited him
and his companion. They arrived at Mooltan, accompanied
by a small escort, and while issuing from the fort gate on
horseback, were murderously assaulted by some of the Governor's men, either at his instigation or by his connivance,
while he galloped off and left them to their fate, both being
eventually killed.

To avenge this foul and dastardly outrage, it was determined to send a large force from Bengal to reduce the town
and fortress, together with a body of Sikh troops furnished by
Punjáb authorities; but the Sikhs, on arrival there, in place of
aiding the British authorities, went over bodily and joined the
rebel enemy with drums beating and banners flying!

42

Such being the serious state of affairs, General Whish felt it his duty to raise the siege and apply for reinforcements.

Accordingly, a strong division of the army from Bombay and Scinde was sent up without delay, of which my regiment formed a part. This force consisted of two European regiments, H.M.'s 60th Rifles, the 1st Bombay Fusiliers, with the 3rd Bombay Native Infantry, 4th Rifles, 9th and 19th Native Infantry, together with artillery and cavalry, etc., forming separate brigades, the whole under the able command of Brigadier-General the Honourable H. Dundas, C.B. (the late Lord Melville).

In the meanwhile, that distinguished frontier officer, Major (afterwards Sir) Herbert Edwardes, with a body of irregular troops aided by the Nawab of Bahawalpore, was very successful by his skill and tact in preventing the insurrection from spreading further.

The Bombay Column left Kurrachee about the beginning of November 1848 in high spirits, and passing through Hyderabad, after many weary and trying marches, reached Roree, the place appointed for the general rendezvous of the force. Here a grand inspection parade took place, on which occasion, being on the regimental staff, I was mounted on a handsome little Arab, which did me good service throughout the campaign. My duties I soon found were by no means light on the line of march, especially under so well-known a martinet as our commanding officer, and much worry and annoyance did they cost me.

The Bombay Division broke up from Roree about the early part of December, and, passing through the Bahawalpore territory, we crossed the Sutlej by a bridge of boats, and reached Mooltan on Christmas Eve. The following day we were inspected and reviewed by General Whish, who expressed himself highly pleased with our appearance.

On the 27th December, at 11 a.m., we commenced operations by attacking the suburbs, which, after a prolonged and severe resistance, we carried in brilliant style. The 60th Rifles were on the extreme right in skirmishing order, and my regiment, the Bombay Rifles, was in similar formation on the left with supports, and our flanks were protected by the Scinde Horse.

As our troops advanced steadily over broken ground, we speedily drove the enemy from their many strong positions— nullahs, stockades, and gardens—succeeding also in capturing the high mound of Seedeelal-Ke bede crowned with guns.

In the meanwhile, however, our skirmishers, in their eagerness having advanced too far, and running short of ammunition, had to fall back on our reserve. We maintained our position till dusk, our guns keeping up a heavy fire from the mound we had captured, and which commanded the town. In this sharp action the casualties in my regiment were greater than those of any other corps engaged.

The clearing of the suburbs so effectually was a most important point gained, as it at once enabled us to renew in good earnest the siege operations, which had been for a time suspended. Thus, in place of having our first parallel at nearly three miles' distance from the fortress (as it was originally), we, two clays after this success, planted two mortar and two breaching batteries within some five hundred yards of it! Subsequently a heavy battery manned by the Indian Navy was planted on the north-west side, and did excellent service throughout the siege.

The city of Mooltan, three miles east of the river Chenab, is one of the most important and populous in the Punjáb. It is upwards of two miles in circumference, and is surmounted by lofty walls of sunburnt bricks, forty feet high, and strengthened by thirty bastions; while the citadel itself, which commands the town, is only divided from it by the glacis and moat encircling it. It is considered one of the most formidable and regularly built fortresses in India.

On 30th December a shell from one of our mortar batteries struck the *Jumma Musjid,* or Great Mosque, and another blew up a powder magazine with a terrific explosion, killing and burying under its ruins, it was reported, nearly one thousand souls, besides causing immense damage to the citadel, stores, etc. Never shall I forget the scene as, rushing out of my tent, I beheld a dark heaving mass rising slowly and imposingly from the interior of the fort, amid dense volumes of smoke, till it reached a vast height, when it assumed the form of a pillar of gigantic proportions, which gradually spreading out became as it were an immense pall hanging mournfully over the doomed fortress, which seemed shaken as by an earthquake. As if by mutual consent, the firing on both sides ceased awhile, everyone gazing upwards with silent awe and wonder! Then from the British camp arose one. loud burst of triumph, which was speedily answered by a furious cannonade from our courageous and still un-subdued enemy.

This catastrophe greatly raised the spirits of the besiegers, and gave such an impetus to the progress of the siege that on the 1st January 1849 the chief engineer reported two breaches of the city walls *practicable*—viz., one near the *Khoonee Boorj* (or Bloody Bastion), and the other near the Delhi Gate; and it was decided that the assault should be delivered the next day. The storming party told off for the former consisted of the Bombay European Fusiliers, the 4th Rifles (my regiment), and the 19th Regiment Native Infantry; for the latter, H.M.'s 32nd Regiment and two Bengal regiments in support. Accordingly, having made all my private arrangements, and given written instructions to my cousin, Colonel B., in case of eventualities, I accompanied my regiment to the rendezvous of our column of attack in rear of the great *Mundee-Ava* Mount. Here we waited in profound silence till 4 p.m., when the signal to storm was given, and immediately the storming party, led by the gallant Brigadier Stalker, boldly advanced at *the double*, on *the deadly breach,* the glorious fusiliers in advance, their forlorn hope being led by the gallant

Captain Leith, while we followed in support, the Sipahees vieing with their European comrades in their struggles to reach the summit amid a shower of bullets, the fire being so intense as to resemble sheet lightning! Twice were the besiegers repulsed with heavy loss, including the heroic Leith, with his equally devoted Subaltern Gray, both of whom were carried off dangerously wounded; while the enemy, growing insolent by their success, planted the green standard of Islam on the crest of the breach in defiance. But the undaunted *Old Toughs* (as the fusiliers were fondly styled), becoming furious at the loss of their officers and their many casualties, with an Irish yell that spread terror and dismay among their foes, and with a loud shout of "Remember Anderson" (their poor murdered officer), rushed up the breach a *third* time, and with desperate energy gained the summit, carrying all before them; while the courageous Colour-Sergeant Bennett, in the midst of a shower of bullets, planted the British colours on the top of the *Bloody Bastion*, and by sunset the bloodstained city of Mooltan was ours!

Then far above the roar of cannon, the sharp rattle of musketry, the groans of the dying and the cries of the wounded, was heard the loud "Hurrah" of British soldiers, mingled with the deafening cheers of their comrades, who with looks of intense anxiety and with straining eyes had watched the deadly conflict to its triumphant issue.

But ah! believe me, kind reader, it is indeed an awful thing to stand thus in the deadly breach, undergoing the baptism of fire, when men are falling on every side, and the same fate may be ours the next moment; and memory, preternaturally quickened, recalls the deeds of the past, the images of friends and relatives far away, and thoughts too deep for utterance of the future and eternity! When one witnesses thus the horrors of war and the misery and suffering it entails, I for one do not envy those fire-eaters who find pleasure in it.

A very tragic affair occurred to a gentleman touring in In-

46

dia, who joined our column as an amateur. Being desirous of seeing something of a siege, he was looking through the loophole of an embrasure, at a comparatively safe distance from the line of fire, watching the storming party mounting the breach, when, unhappily, a stray shot pierced his brain! It was a truly sad catastrophe. *Mais que diable allait-il faire dans cette galère!*

But to return to my narrative—for more work was in store for us. The Bengal Column were unable to effect an entrance from the Delhi Gate owing to the imperfect breach, but they came into the city by the one we had won, and aided us in clearing the streets of the town. This was no easy or pleasant task, as we had to run the gauntlet of a heavy fire from the tall houses and other buildings on either side, which caused us some loss. Our doctor—a tall, prominent figure with a long beard—(to whom I was talking at the time) had a narrow escape, a bullet having pierced his ear close to his temple, and he quietly remarked, "This is rather a warm corner!" and leisurely moved away; not, however, without our inflicting punishment on the offenders.

Driving the enemy before us, and passing through the *Chowk*, or Grain Market, which was strewn with many of the slain, mostly Sikhs, we reached the Loharee Gate, where we bivouacked for the night, first taking the precaution of planting a chain of double sentries all around to prevent surprise.

Exhausted with the fatigues of such a day's work, we—that is, the Headquarters of regiments and their staff—lay on the ground, and, though worn out, few of us closed an eye, from the sense of danger still surrounding us. An ominous silence prevailed, broken only by a stray shot or the hoarse challenge of a sentry. But about midnight a cry was heard, followed by the terrific explosion of a powder magazine in our immediate vicinity, causing the houses to rock and fall, burying many of our men beneath their ruins.

All of us started up at once, fearing a mine had been sprung, and that we should momentarily be attacked ; but, happily for

47

us, no such attack was attempted. Never shall I forget the fearful scene, which is indelibly impressed on my mind. Amid the shouts of officers earnestly calling upon their men to "Be steady and stand to your arms" were heard the heart-piercing cries and groans of those buried alive, imploring to be released from their sufferings, while here and there amid the glare the glimpse of a ghastly hand or outstretched limb would be seen protruding from the debris. It was with great difficulty and labour that we at length managed to rescue some of the victims; but, alas! ten were killed and thirty otherwise injured of my regiment. I myself had rather a narrow escape, as I was lying on a native cot close up to the walls when I felt myself lifted up by the force of the explosion and thrown down violently with the cot providentially over me, for it served as a screen from the bricks and earth which fell around me, so that I escaped, though stunned and shaken. It was never ascertained whether this explosion was by accident or design.

Next morning, to our great joy, we were relieved by the 60th Rifles and a native regiment, and on reaching my tent I—like, doubtless, many others— offered up heart-felt thanksgivings to "Him who holdeth our soul in life" for His merciful protection in the midst of so many and great dangers.

The conduct of our troops on capturing the city was most exemplary, as there were no outrages or looting to any extent; and few cities taken by storm have been treated with such forbearance. A hospital was also established in the town for the wounded and sick of the enemy, who had been entirely neglected by their own brethren.

The town being now in our possession, we were enabled at once to turn our attention to the citadel where the Governor Moolraj with the remnant of his army had shut himself up, and still held out. One of their unexploded brass shells weighing 87 lbs. fell near my cousin's tent, who quietly appropriated it, and brought it home to England as a trophy, and it is now in the possession of his son.

By the 20th January 1849 two breaches were reported practicable, and the storming parties told off (one of which was commanded by my cousin) to be in readiness to storm the citadel next clay. But reduced to the last extremity, and having had ocular proofs of the determined spirit of his assailants, the heart of the Governor failed him, and he surrendered unconditionally. Accordingly, on the morning of the 22nd January 1849, amid a storm of thunder and rain, and when the storming party was actually in position, he and all his garrison marched out and laid down their arms before the British columns drawn up on the glacis. The Governor was made a state prisoner for complicity in the murder of Messrs. Agnew and Anderson. It was an imposing sight, and a proud moment for the victors. Thus ended the memorable siege of Mooltan, in which our casualties were, I believe, about twelve hundred.

No less a distinguished authority than the late Field-Marshal Sir John Burgoyne (who has been styled the Moltke of the British Army) bore the highest testimony to the skill and ability of the engineers, Sir John Cheape and Captain Napier (afterwards of Magdala), and to the masterly manner in which the siege operations had been successfully carried out.

CHAPTER 6

After the Siege

Immediately after the happy termination of the siege of Mooltan, a garrison of Bombay troops was left there (which included, to our great disgust, my own regiment), the remainder of the large force proceeding by forced marches to join Lord Gough's army of the Punjab.

Previous, however, to their departure, a solemn and sacred duty was performed, which could hardly fail to produce a deep impression not only on the inhabitants but also on all who witnessed the affecting scene. The bodies of our poor murdered countrymen were removed with the utmost care, and conveyed by a party of the fusiliers (Anderson's own regiment) to ground consecrated for the purpose, where they received Christian burial. The impressive funeral service of the Church of England was read by the chaplain in presence of a large concourse of officers and soldiers in uniform, who there assembled to pay their last mark of respect to the memory of the dead. An obelisk recording this sad tragedy has since been erected on the site where it occurred.

It was indeed fortunate for the welfare and destinies of India that this siege was brought to so speedy a close, for at this period the army of the Commander-in-Chief, Lord Gough, was in a very critical position, having had two engagements (Ramnuggur and Chillianwalla) with the Sikh Army assisted by the Afghans, in which we had sustained severe loss and repulse.

By the timely arrival, however, of these reinforcements the Commander-in-Chief was enabled, on the 21st February 1849, to fight the battle of Goojerat. The enemy, numbering sixty thousand men, with an immense number of guns were signally defeated, being-pursued to the banks of the Jhelum, and fourteen thousand men with many guns were compelled to lay down their arms before their conquerors! This glorious success resulted, as I have said, in the annexation to British territory of the Punjáb, the country of the five rivers.

Thus ended the second Punjáb war, in commemoration of which a medal (with clasps) was awarded by Her Gracious Majesty, together with six months' *batta*, or extra pay, to her loyal and devoted Army.

This fertile Province of the Punjáb, on the northern frontiers of India, by the masterly administration of the Lawrence brothers and other eminent men, proved, humanly speaking, the salvation of our Empire during the crisis of the Great Indian Mutiny a few years later. From it were promptly forwarded excellent troops trained by such splendid officers as Nicholson, Chamberlain, and Daly, to the siege of Delhi, before the arrival of the great body of British troops from England. All honour to these great men!

That noble Christian soldier, Sir Henry Lawrence (whom I had once the privilege of seeing), the heroic defender of Lucknow and the founder of the Lawrence Orphanage for soldiers' children, when dying ordered the following simple and pathetic words to be placed on his tomb:

Here lies Henry Lawrence
Who tried to do his duty

The prospect of those whose fate it was to garrison Mooltan was far from pleasing or encouraging, for the place was proverbial in the East for "heat, dust, and flies"! Moreover, it was notoriously unhealthy, as the malaria arising from the inundations of the river by which the plains were submerged was great; besides which, there were the horrible effluvia from bodies dug up by the prize agents when searching for hidden treasure (a practice speedily put a stop to), as well as from the dead lying unburied outside the fort. The foul work of clearing the latter away was mostly left to the vultures and pariah dogs. It was indeed a sickening sight to see these scavengers at work, and it forcibly brought to my mind Byron's powerful lines on *The Siege of Corinth*—

And he saw the lean dogs beneath the wall
Hold o'er the dead their carnival,
Gorging and growling o'er carcass and limb,
They were too busy to bark at him!
From a Tartar's skull they had stripp'd the flesh,
As you peel the fig when the fruit is fresh,
As they lazily mumbled the bones of the dead!

Perhaps, however, it saved us from a pestilence.

My regiment was for some time encamped outside the town, the heat being often intense, the thermometer in tents ranging from 100° to 105°; and eventually, owing to the inundations, we were compelled to seek refuge in the fort itself, where, through the kindness of my cousin (who was commanding his regiment there), I obtained the shelter of a small brick dome adjoining his own and under the big flagstaff mount.

Previous to this, however, an act of stern justice had been performed by the summary trial and execution of the infamous Goojar Sing, the murderer of poor Anderson. I was present on this occasion, being on duty with a party of our men, who with loaded arms acted as guard, and certainly I was amazed at the sang-froid of the guilty wretch, who, with hands tied behind his back and muttering some form of incantation or prayer, quietly walked to the gallows, up a narrow plank placed at an angle of nearly 40°, unassisted, a feat difficult to accomplish even without the fear of violent death before one!

The town of Mooltan, with some seventy thousand inhabitants, paid high honours to this murderer, and it was thought that it would have been a fitting punishment to have held it to ransom, and to have divided the money among the troops engaged; but the Government, I presume, thought it would paralyse its trade, which is considerable, being a large commercial centre. It is celebrated for its manufactures of silks, shawls, brocades, and scarves. Some of the latter, beautifully dyed in various delicate colours, I sent home, and they were much admired; also, by way of souvenirs of the siege, I got a fine ivory-handled dagger with Damascene blade, and a handsome Durbar robe of cashmere cloth.

The life we led at Mooltan for some months was dreary and dismal, with little to relieve its monotony; however, on one occasion I obtained a few days' leave, and with a brother officer proceeded to a garden on the banks of the Chenab, where we amused ourselves with rifle practice and hawking. This latter sport was novel to us, so we accepted the invitation of a *zumeendar*, or landowner, to accompany him, which we did on horseback, a somewhat risky proceeding, for while gazing upwards and galloping forward to keep in sight of the *quarry*, we ran a good chance of coming to grief through the roughness of the ground when watching the poor little victim of a partridge uttering shrill cries of terror as it vainly sought to escape the *fell swoop*!

North of the town is the famous Mohammedan shrine of *Shums Tabreez,* or Blue Mosque, in the neighbourhood of which are several fine gardens. Though the country around is somewhat tame, yet it contains various fruit trees, such as pomegranates, oranges and apples, with grain in abundance; while from the top of a mosque or minaret inside the fort a fine view is obtained of the snow-capped *Tukt-i Sooliman* (Throne of Solomon), a high peak, "which seems the very clouds to kiss," of the Sooliman range of the mighty Himalayas.

An interesting ceremony took place at this time in the

presentation to a *havildar*, or native sergeant, of my regiment of a medal of the Order of Merit, conferred upon him by the Commander-in-Chief for conspicuous bravery at the siege. The garrison was formed into a square, and it fell to my duty as interpreter to convey to the man in Hindustani the words of commendation of the Commander-in-Chief as well as the commanding officer, after which the Brigadier pinned the medal to his breast, and the troops saluted and marched past. This brave soldier, by name Ram Sing, was subsequently promoted to be a native officer.

About the months of August and September the heat became almost insupportable, and the sickness was so great that there were few who were not prostrated by fever, and we lost many men, including one of our captains, who was much liked and regretted. In fact, matters became so serious that the Brigadier on his own responsibility sent the European Artillery down the river to Kurrachee. Several officers suffered from fever, including my cousin, Colonel B., who was invalided, and I myself also had fever, and one day fainted from weakness in my bathroom.

However, during this weary time I managed to continue my study of the Mahrattee language, and at length applied for and obtained leave to proceed to Bombay for the Presidency examination.

Accordingly, towards the close of the year, I left Mooltan without regret, and in company with a friend of the Bombay Lancers, bent on a similar errand, we sailed rapidly down the river Chenab, amusing ourselves *en passant* in shooting alligators and pelicans. We duly reached Sukkur, where, to our disgust, we found letters awaiting us from the Brigade Major at Mooltan desiring us to "stand fast till further orders," as the garrison there were about to be relieved. This was most provoking, as we feared we should be too late for the examination. However, through the kindness and hospitality of our friends, we passed nearly a month there pleasantly enough, and were then permitted to proceed, duly arriving at Bombay early the following year, but too late for the presidency examination.

I pitched my tent on the esplanade, and again set to work with the aid of an able *pundit*, or teacher in the Mahrattee lingo, and was confidently assured by him that in a month's time I should be quite ready to pass. My friend and I then applied for and obtained, under the circumstances, a special examination, when we both successfully passed the ordeal and in due time I had the satisfaction of seeing my name in General Orders confirming my appointment as quartermaster, paymaster, and interpreter to my regiment.

Soon after I left Bombay and joined my regiment at Belgaum, where I also had the pleasure of meeting again my cousin, who was in command of his regiment at that place. Belgaum is a healthy and favourite station, and the country around abounds with game. The place itself has a most attractive appearance, every house having a nice garden; while the town boasts a public library, a race-course, and pleasant society.

Here on one occasion I witnessed a fight between a panther and two elephants, got up by a neighbouring Rajah, which attracted an immense concourse of people and ended in a tragic manner. It took place on the parade ground, a large iron stake being driven into the ground, to which the panther was fastened by an iron chain. On the elephants approaching, he made a sudden and tremendous spring upon one of them, and in so doing broke the chain. Consternation ensued, and *sauve qui peut* was the order of the day! The elephants bolted, causing serious injury to some; while the panther disposed of one or two natives and slightly mauled a European officer before it was eventually killed.

My bungalow was a good one with a nice garden, and expecting to remain some time here, I had treated myself to a buggy (or gig); but finding I could not shake off the Mooltan fever, and that I was growing weaker and thinner, our worthy doctor decided at length on sending me to Bombay on sick certificate. Accordingly, disposing of all my kit, horses, etc., and taking leave of my friends, I proceeded to the Ram Ghaut (where, by the way, on my previous visit I lost a beautiful Surat goat, which was carried off by a cheetah), and duly reaching Bombay, put up at the sanatorium for sick officers. Here after a month's stay I passed the Medical Board and obtained a medical certificate to visit Europe for three years— joyful news to the weary Indian exile *homeward bound!*

The setting sun was sinking like a ball of fire and tinging the western horizon with a golden hue as we steamed out of Bombay harbour on the 2nd November 1850, amid the good wishes of our friends for a *bon voyage.*

It was not till we were well out of sight of land that I fully realised we were actually homeward bound, and what with the exhilarating thought of soon meeting my beloved relatives and friends after an absence of about seven years (the usual term of transportation), together with the refreshing sea-breezes, my health and spirits gradually revived in spite of ague and fever. I duly reached London early in June 1851, thankful to be back once more in dear old England.

CHAPTER 7

Round the Cape

The period of my furlough having now nearly expired, and having paid my farewell round of visits, I commenced preparations for my second departure for India, whither, by way of a change and on the score of economy, I decided on going *viâ* the Cape. The last parting glass of sparkling champagne had been quaffed, the last affectionate adieu had been uttered, the last hand-clasp given, when on the deck of the *Seringapatam,* East Indiaman (commanded by Captain Gimlett), I found myself alone, entirely among strangers. There were some 50 passengers, with about 150 recruits for H.M.'s 5th and 85th Regiments at the Mauritius, under command of Major Simmons, making with the crew and officers a total of nearly 250 persons.

It was a lovely afternoon in the early part of July 1854 that we dropped down the Thames. In due time we ran close under the Isle of Wight, and lay becalmed off the Bill of Portland, it being a beautiful moonlight night. The following morning (Sunday), the Rev. Mr. Laseron, a missionary, performed divine service on deck to a very attentive audience, and the same night the pilot left us abreast the start on the Devonshire coast. As the shores of dear old England gradually receded from our gaze, we felt indeed that we were fairly off on our long voyage across the broad Atlantic, and by more than one heart was breathed a prayer for preservation from the perils of the mighty deep.

As I kept a journal of our voyage, I extract such items as are of some interest.

10th July.—We have now fairly settled down. My fellow-passengers are an agreeable set, and we have every prospect of a pleasant voyage. *Mais l'homme propose et Dieu dispose.* We have prayers, I'm glad to find, morning and evening. Passing several vessels in the Channel, we soon entered the Bay of Biscay, and were off Cape Finisterre on the 15th; sighted the beautiful island of Madeira, the Canaries, and entered the tropics on the 24th.

29th.—Becalmed. Watched the Bonitos chasing the poor flying-fish. Some of the latter flew on deck to escape, but came "out of the frying-pan into the fire." Had some rifle practice on some black fish who were sporting near us.

8th August.—Crossed the line! Father Neptune, attended by his satellites, made his appearance, and performed the usual unpleasant shaving process, which we officers escaped by paying a ransom, though some of the ship's crew were victimised. Signalled a large screw steamer. The captain pointed out to me the fine constellation of the Southern Cross.

14th August.—Abreast of St. Helena, though a long way off. This evening we performed with great éclat the play of *The Bachelor of Arts,* in which I took a part, Dr. Tulloch eliciting much applause by his excellent acting. On the fine nights in the tropics, when we were scudding through the waters, the soldiers were very fond of singing songs with good choruses; and as there were among them some really superior singers, we used greatly to enjoy their performances.

On the 21st we had a splendid run of 216 miles; but for several subsequent days heavy gales prevailed, the ship rolling tremendously, and sea-pies the order of the day, as no cooking could be performed.

31st.—Nearly becalmed. The captain went out in his boat to examine the state of the vessel after the late heavy gales she had encountered, and found that a large piece of coppering from her bottom had been torn off. A splendid albatross was shot by the captain, measuring, from tip to tip of the wings, 10 feet. This, by the way, was a strange thing for a sailor to do, and in the light of subsequent events it reminded me of the superstitions of Coleridge's *Ancient Mariner*.

4th September.—Spoke the brig *Abeona* bound for Hong Kong; and, most singular to relate, on that same afternoon it came across the famous *sea-serpent*; and thus, it maybe, we missed the chance by a few hours of seeing one of the world's wonders. An account of this rare phenomenon appeared in the *Friend of India* newspaper, which I here transcribe.

Captain Richardson of the brig *Abeona* has favoured us with a curious and interesting memorandum of his rencontre with the great sea-serpent. He writes:

On the 4th September, in lat. 38° 15 south, long. 12° 55 east, about 350 miles and west of the Cape of Good Hope, spoke the ship *Seringapatam* bound for Bombay all well; same day about 5 p.m. saw broken water on the weather quarter, and presently the head of an enormous sea-monster appeared about 30 feet above the water. The head was long and narrow, eyes not visible, from the tip of the nose about 12 feet, on each side of the breast there was a white streak about a foot wide, which I supposed to be his mouth. About 6 feet from the end of the white streak (or jaw) there was a large hump on his back; his body at the surface of the water was about the size round of the long boat. Underneath the jaws there appeared to be a quantity of shock (tawny) hair, like the pouch of a pelican—it was of a lighter colour than the rest of the body, which appeared black and smooth. He appeared to be about 180 feet long, *as near as I could judge.* The water broke in several places along his body, which I think must have been occasioned by humps similar to the one close to his head. He was about three ships' lengths from us, and was visible for about sixteen minutes. He kept moving his head from side to side, and made a serpentine course through the water, keeping way with the vessel, when he suddenly disappeared, and we saw him no more. I have not the slightest hesitation in saying that it was the celebrated sea-serpent which I believe was last seen by the officers of H.M.S. *Dædalus* somewhere between the Cape of Good Hope and St. Helena in 1849-50.

For my part, I quite believe in the existence of the sea-serpent, seeing also that special mention is made of it in the Scriptures.

5th September.—Last night during the middle watch a most melancholy accident occurred: one of the seamen was killed, having fallen on the lower deck from the maintop-gallant yard. Early this morning the poor fellow's remains were consigned to the deep, the troops parading and officers in uniform, while the Rev. E. Laseron read the sublime and impressive burial service. We have now rounded the Cape, having cleared Cape Agulhas.

6th September.—*Last* night the vessel pitched and strained heavily, owing to the tremendous sea, which, to our dismay, caused her to spring several leaks; and it will be a serious matter if we encounter any very rough weather. Pumps are in frequent requisition, and the ship pronounced by those qualified to judge to be unseaworthy from her age.

11th September.—We are now at the mouth of the dreaded Mozambique Channel, but are making little progress, owing to the leaky condition of the ship, which prevents us from putting her under full sail, however favourable the wind may be.

13th September.—A heavy gale of wind during the day, which increased to a fearful storm or typhoon in the course, to us, of this ever-memorable and awful night. Never so long as I live shall I forget it, and indeed those only who have ever been similarly situated can fully realise it, and it is difficult in words to convey any adequate conception of its horrors.

Let me try to picture the scene. There was profound darkness, broken only by the awful glare of the lightning, followed by terrific peals of thunder. Torrents of rain were descending, the wind howled, and the angry foaming waves rose like a wall around us, as though eager to engulf their helpless prey. The vessel strained and leaked fearfully, though the pumps were kept hard at work. Amid the raging storm our frail barque was driven helplessly before the wind. Our situation was now truly deplorable, for we felt that if it continued much longer the vessel must founder. When the storm was at its height a little before midnight I overheard the captain say in confidence to the chief officer, "Nothing human can save us; we must bear it like men!" Nought indeed now remained for us but to invoke the mighty aid of *Him* who ruleth the raging of the sea," and some of us assembled in the cabin of Mrs. B., a truly Christian lady (as was shown by her calmness and resignation in this trying hour), where we all earnestly wrestled in prayer to Almighty God, and read the beautiful 107th Psalm, so appropriate to our present circumstances. With what power did those inspired words come home to our hearts at such a time: "Then they cry unto the Lord in their trouble, and He bringeth them out of their distresses." Such was in truth our exact situation, and God was pleased to answer our earnest prayers for deliverance from the very jaws of death in a remarkable manner; for suddenly, after one of the most terrific peals of thunder I ever heard, the storm ceased as if by a miracle, the winds were hushed, the sea became as calm as our own dear Windermere, the rain ceased, and the stars shone out bright above us. How truly did we realise then those words of the Psalmist: "He maketh the storm a calm, and the waves thereof are still. Then are they glad because they be quiet; so He bringeth them to their desired haven."When we perceived this gracious manifestation of the divine goodness, we did not fail to offer up our united heart-felt thanks for so wonderful a preservation.

But though we had thus through God's mercy escaped *imminent* danger, our situation was still very critical, and our only chance, humanly speaking, lay in lightening the ship as much as possible, endeavouring to stop the principal leak in some measure, keeping the pumps in constant use, and relying on providence to send us favourable winds and moderate weather.

Accordingly, we threw overboard nearly two hundred tons of railway iron and other miscellaneous. cargo, together with the heavy guns or carronades she carried, keeping one to be used for signals of distress. At this critical juncture, to add to our difficulties, the wretched sailors, when throwing the cargo overboard, broached some cases of brandy, and became mad with drink, and exhibited a mutinous spirit, saying it was useless to save the d——d old ship, and that "when matters came to the worst, Jack was as good as his master!" It required all the captain's firmness and presence of mind, backed by his officers armed with revolvers, to make these mutineers give up the bottles they had secreted in their hammocks.

Our soldiers, though only recruits, behaved very well, and together with their officers and passengers were formed into gangs to work the pumps in turn, day and night, which we found very exhausting.

Providentially, the weather was favourable, and hope sprung in our hearts that we might yet be spared to reach our destination. I have lately at night, when gazing at the starry firmament in a serious mood, been particularly struck by noticing, *amid the glittering host* bestudding this southern sky, one particularly bright star immediately overhead, which seems to be watching over us; and it has vividly recalled to my mind a favourite hymn by Kirke White—

Once on the raging seas I rode,
The storm was loud, the night was dark,
The ocean yawned, and rudely blow'd
The wind that tossed our found'ring bark.
Deep horror then my vitals froze,
Death-struck I ceas'd the tide to stem,
When suddenly a star arose,
It was the Star of Bethlehem !

It was my guide, my light, my all,
It bade my dark forebodings cease,
And thro' the storm, and danger's thrall,
It led me to the port of peace!

20th September.—We have made a good run, the wind being highly favourable, though the sea is rather high. A paper has been drawn up by Captain Kelly, R.N., one of our passengers, containing a simple statement of facts reflecting strongly on the owners of the vessel in sending her to sea in so unseaworthy a state, which document all the passengers have signed, and it will be published in the Mauritius, Indian, and London papers.

24th September.—We are now within a hundred miles of the Mauritius, and just before sunset, to our great joy, we sighted *La belle Maurice*, and the following morning passed Round Island and La Gabrielle, when a pilot came on board, who informed us that a terrible scourge of cholera had recently decimated the population, but happily had now nearly disappeared.

As we approached Port Louis we enjoyed a fine panoramic view of this picturesque island, with its luxuriant green sugarcane plantations, which skirt the shore, and the same afternoon safely anchored there. Many boats containing friends came out to us, and when they heard our story, and saw the very disabled condition of the vessel, they wondered that we ever reached land at all.

On landing I proceeded to the *Hôtel de L'Europe*, and never did I set foot on *terra firma* with a greater feeling of thankfulness to the Almighty. God grant that the remembrance of our great deliverance may never be effaced from our hearts and memories!

CHAPTER 8

Mauritius and Ceylon

From the hotel at Port Louis I wrote to an old friend, who speedily made his appearance and invited me to his house on *La Grande Riviere*, which cordial offer I gratefully accepted. Nearly all my fellow-passengers were comfortably accommodated by the hospitable inhabitants, who evinced much kindness and sympathy towards us. The passengers for Bombay were informed by the captain and agents that measures would be taken as early as possible to forward us to our destination. I may here mention that the ringleaders of the *émeute* on board the *Seringapatam* were convicted and sentenced to various terms of imprisonment with hard labour. Both the captain and chief officer, in their evidence before the Courts, deposed that the vessel had been "in a sinking state for several days." During this enforced detention I amused myself by making excursions into the interior of this fine and highly cultivated island. I was also made an Honorary Member of the mess of the 5th Fusiliers, through the kindness of an officer of that crack regiment who was also a fellow-passenger of mine.

I was invited by another friend to pay a visit to his sugar plantation situated at the foot of some mountains, and was duly initiated into the mysteries of sugar-making and boiling down, in which I observed many Indian *coolies* were employed, and found very useful.

The island of Bourbon, about a hundred miles distant, is

said to be richer and more productive than the Mauritius. Some of our Indian regiments (mine among the number) were present at the capture of this island from the French, crossing bayonets with them, and they now bear on their appointments the word "Bourbon." It was, however, restored to the French at the general peace in 1815.

The principal event during my *séjour* at Mauritius was the races held in the Champs de Mars, which created great excitement, and where all the beauty and fashion were congregated and dressed in the highest Parisian style. I was greatly amused to see among them many negresses imitating the Creole ladies (many of the latter being good-looking and graceful), gorgeously bedecked in all the colours of the rainbow, with Parisian bonnets over their woolly, matted hair plastered clown with coconut oil, bright pink dresses, green parasols adorned with naming paroquets, brooches of imitation gold as large as a cheese-plate, huge watches and chains, white kid gloves, and *bare* feet! They evidently thought themselves quite *à la mode!*

The little Mauritius world is of a somewhat heterogeneous character, for here are assembled English, French, Germans, Creoles, Arabs, Chinese, Indians, and natives of Madagascar (called Malagash), and other tribes.

I occasionally drove out or rode on my friend's sturdy, active Pegu pony along the Pampelouse road or other favourite resorts, and also went with a picnic party to visit the spot where tradition avers those two lovers, Paul and Virginia, "faithful unto death," were laid to rest.

I had now been nearly a month at the Mauritius, and seeing that there was no *early* prospect of our being forwarded by the ship's agents to our destination, and not wishing further to tax the hospitality of my kind friend—and finding, moreover, by the Indian papers that the regimental appointment which I held before leaving India had become vacant, and could be claimed by me—I decided to leave on the first opportunity. Accordingly, learning that the French barque *Mahé de la Bour-*

donnais was about to sail for Ceylon with the mails, I at once took my passage in her, with the intention of catching the P. & O. steamer at Galle on its way to Bombay from China.

On the 21st October, after a farewell tiffin with my friend, the Governor's A.D.C., I bade adieu to the Mauritius, passing, as we left the harbour, close to the poor old disabled *Seringapatam*.

The only passengers on board the French ship beside myself were the captain's wife and child, my friend and fellow-passenger from England (Dr. Tulloch), and a French Vicomte, with whom I fraternised, and improved my French by reading Madame de Stael's interesting novel of *Corinne,* which he presented me with.

One of the ship's officers sang in French remarkably well, and I was much touched by one song with the pathetic lament to his mother of a poor little cabin-boy who was consigned to the tender mercies of a brutal captain, and the refrain of which was:

"Ah! ma mere qu'as tu fait de ton petit?"

which he sang with much feeling and pathos.

Nothing worthy of particular note occurred during the voyage, but as we approached the entrance to Galle we were within an ace of again coming to grief by striking on some sunken rocks, the *breakers* being close ahead!

Providentially, we were warned off *just in time* by some natives in a boat, who, seeing our danger, made wild and frantic signals and gesticulations to apprise us of the same, and we had only just room to veer round! The pilot soon after came on board, and told us we had had a narrow escape, for the approach to Galle is intricate and dangerous, and many sharks on this coast, as he grimly told us.

We arrived at Galle on the 11th November, after about a three weeks' voyage, and put up at the Mansion House Hotel. In the evening the captain, his wife, and ourselves dined there together, and a pleasant evening was passed. The news of the glorious battle of the Alma and utter defeat of the Russians had just reached us, and various toasts were proposed and drunk in honour of the allied armies, and cordially responded to. The next day being Sunday, I went to the chapel which had been built by the Dutch when occupied by them, and which contains a fine monument to one of their former Governors. The clergyman in his sermon, when enlarging on the benefits and consolations of religion, read an extract from a letter he had received from the seat of war in the Crimea, giving an interesting account of the administration of the Holy Communion to the British Army just before their engagement with the Russians. "It was" (he read) "under the broad canopy of heaven. The regiments formed into an immense hollow square, a rude table in the centre, generals, officers, and men all humbly kneeling side by side on the green sward." It must have been indeed a touching and impressive sight!

Galle, or Point de Galle, from its geographical position, is a place of some importance, having a secure harbour, etc. Mail steamers and other vessels from India and China touch here. It has a strong fort built by the Dutch, which was at this time garrisoned by some companies of the Ceylon Rifles, whose uniform and organisation is much similar to that of our Indian rifle regiments, having native as well as European officers.

During my short stay in Ceylon I made some little excursions into the interior. On one occasion I drove to a villa which was a favourite place for picnics, being beautifully situated ; the view of the Haycock range of mountains, with the celebrated Adam's Peak towering over all, is particularly fine, while in front flows a winding river whose banks are fringed by a thick forest of coconut and palm trees.

I also visited the far-famed Cinnamon Gardens, which also contain coffee, mace, cloves, and other spices, and carried off, by way of souvenirs, several walking-sticks of cinnamon, whose bark is pleasant to the taste. I purchased a few curios in the shape of precious stones, tortoise-shell ornaments, paperweights of elephants' teeth, etc.; but much caution is required to deal with these natives, as they are sad rogues. A pearl fishery exists here, and several natives volunteered to dive down at once, and bring up pearls, which they offered for sale ; but of course it was a fraud, as they had them secreted about their persons.

On our way home we peeped into a Buddhist temple, which I found to be very like the Hindoo ones, with some hideous idols within. There are many Buddhists who venerate Buddha's great tooth, which the late eminent Professor Owen is said to have pronounced to be that of an animal! It may be well to mention that this sacred tooth of Gautama, which is preserved at Kandy, is guarded with jealous care and preserved in an elegant shrine. But good authorities state that the original relic was destroyed by the Portuguese, and that the present tooth is only a piece of discoloured ivory, which bears no resemblance to a human tooth.

The elephants of Ceylon are very fine, and much used as beasts of burden, especially the Government ones, which are well trained; and I was much interested in watching them lift immense weights and arranging great logs in due order as directed by the Mahout, showing remarkable skill, docility, and intelligence.

One evening I took a walk along the ramparts, and ascended the lighthouse, built of cast-iron on a solid rock, from the top of which there is a very fine view.

The Cingalese are an intelligent but somewhat singular and effeminate-looking race, and the dress of the men is so very similar to that of the women, wearing petticoats, and even tortoise-shell, combs in their hair, that it is very difficult to distinguish those who are young and beardless from the weaker sex.

On the 16th November I bade farewell to Ceylon and embarked on board the P. & O. Co.'s steamer *Erin,* which I found very comfortable. There were several passengers from China, including Parsees, who are very intelligent and enterprising.

On the following day we sighted Cape Comorin, the most southern point of India, and then steaming along the Malabar coast, which was plainly visible, we passed by Quilon, Cochin, Calicut, etc., the great Western Ghauts—the backbone of India—extending parallel to the coast. In the afternoon we came abreast of the old Portuguese settlement of Goa.

On the following morning we came in sight of Bombay, with its many picturesque islands, and landed about 3 p.m. I was truly glad and thankful to have got safe to my destination. I may here mention that our steamer the *Erin* proved ill-fated subsequently when in 1857, conveying General Havelock and others to Calcutta during the height of the Mutiny, she was wrecked off the coast of Ceylon, near Galle, and it was with difficulty that the passengers and crew were saved.

One of the first persons I saw on land was, to my great surprise, my old native servant and factotum, who greeted me with a low salaam and a broad grin of recognition and welcome. It seems he had learnt from my brother officers that I was expected about that time, and met every steamer that arrived till he found me! He then, without any hint from me, coolly assumed the sole charge of myself and baggage, as though I had been away a few days only, instead of some years!

I was, however, very glad to secure his services again, as he was one of the most honest and trustworthy creatures I ever met in India or elsewhere.

I preferred at once a claim on the owners of the *Seringapatam* for the recovery of part of my passage money, which was granted; while my less fortunate fellow-passengers, who were detained for months, and put to great expense at the Mauritius, did not arrive at their destination till upwards of two months. So I *scored* on this occasion.

After a kind reception from my Bombay friends, with

whom I stayed some days, I proceeded to Poona to rejoin my regiment, and was cordially received by the Colonel and others.

The next day I was formally installed in my old regimental appointment, and found myself fairly in harness again after my long holiday.

Since leaving the regiment I found that many changes had taken place, it having suffered much from that dreadful scourge the cholera, so that I was now Senior Lieutenant, and ready for my promotion, which was not long in coming, as will appear by the next chapter.

CHAPTER 9

Promotion and Tiger-Hunting

Poona, once the ancient capital of the Mahratta Empire of the Peishwa, is the largest cantonment in the Western Presidency, and, owing to its salubrity and proximity to the hills and Bombay, is a favourite and gay station. There is a fine view of the city and cantonment from the adjacent Parbuttee Hill, from the summit of which, ascended by a flight of many steps, is the Hindoo temple dedicated to the goddess of that name, who is much revered by these idol-worshippers.

At this period Poona was a large camp of exercise, something like our Chobham, while drills, parades, and grand field-days were the order of the day, our energetic commanding officer giving us little rest.

We had, however, the satisfaction of obtaining the character of being one of the best-drilled corps in the Indian Army, and the Commander-in-Chief, General Sir H. Somerset, K.C.B., at our annual inspection spoke in the very highest terms of the regiment (the Rifles), which was very gratifying to all ranks.

Among the troops composing the Poona Division was the gallant 78th Highlanders, who specially distinguished themselves at Lucknow, and during: the Mutiny being styled *Havelock's Pets*. Two of my friends among the officers were unhappily killed at Lucknow.

On New Year's Day 1855 at muster parade I read the *Articles of War* to my regiment, and in the afternoon rode to

Kirkee and mustered H.M.'s 10th Hussars, who were under orders to go to the seat of war in the Crimea by the overland route. The news of the glorious but bloody battle of Inkerman had just reached us.

2nd January was the anniversary of the storm and capture of Mooltan, in honour of which event my regiment, having taken an active part, gave a *Burra Khana*, or grand dinner, to the station, which went off with great eclat.

A college had recently been established at Poona, by the Commander-in-Chief, for the purpose of instructing officers in military surveying and engineering, and encouragement was held out by the authorities to those who qualified themselves. I applied, and obtained permission to join it, relinquishing temporarily my regimental staff appointment, and in due time passed the examination, my name appearing in *General Orders* as being qualified.

In September 1855 I had the great satisfaction of being promoted to the rank of Captain, and it was a source of no small gratification to be released from the drudgery of a regimental subaltern's duties.

Soon after my promotion, and being qualified as a surveyor, I was offered an appointment by my kind friend the Honourable Mr. Reeves, a member of the Council in the *Revenue Survey*; but finding that I should have to serve in that department under an officer who was my junior in the army, I declined it, especially as I still held the interpretership of regiment.

About the end of April 1856 I obtained a month leave, and proceeded, in company with a brother officer, *viâ* Sattara to the Mahabuleshwur Hills, a favourite resort of mine, both for its cool, salubrious climate, fine scenery, and good sport for big game. We found our tent pitched there, as it had been sent on ahead with our baggage, etc.

I here made the acquaintance of two eminent Christian gentlemen, Dr. Wilson—a great Oriental scholar and author of *The Lands of the Bible*—and Major Molesworth, compiler of the *Mahratta Dictionary*, who had also a wonderful knowledge of the Scriptures.

While at the hills I met Captain Elliot, the A.D.C. of His Excellency the Governor of Bombay, a very keen though reckless sportsman, who had a miraculous escape from literally the very jaws of a tiger when out shooting with his friend Captain Rice (who saved his life), as graphically related in the latter's book on *Tiger-Shooting in India*.

Elliot told me the story. He said that he had wounded a tiger, and wishing to follow up the *pugs*, descended from his perch on a tree, a most risky and highly dangerous action, and was looking for the traces of blood, when suddenly the tiger, with a tremendous roar, sprang upon him from higher ground. Instinctively he threw up his rifle for protection, which providentially saved his head; and the animal, seizing him by the arm, carried him off as a cat would a mouse! Captain Rice, who was a man of great nerve, calmly levelled his gun, but was at first unable to fire, Elliot's head being in the way; but, seeing it droop, he fired, and by a splendid shot killed the tiger, and found it stone-dead, with poor E., who had fainted, lying beside it! On his recovery, a litter of branches of trees was improvised by the beaters, as well as another for the tiger. He told me that long afterwards he was haunted with the horrid vision of this striped monster, from whose jaws he had so narrowly escaped, being carried for miles alongside of him, and he too weak to say anything! He eventually went home on sick certificate, but his arm was much shattered and bent. One would imagine that after such a fearful experience he would have given tigers a wide berth; but, on the contrary, on his return to India after his recovery, he swore eternal enmity to tigers generally, and learning that a terrible man-eating tigress had appeared in the Kolnar valley below, and that she had killed and eaten many of the inhabitants of a village there, which had become nearly deserted, and that Government had offered a large reward for its destruction, he at once organised a tiger-shooting party, and persuaded my chum and myself to join it, making altogether five of us, while our friends pronounced the affair a most foolhardy undertaking.

We started about the middle of May, and made Elliot our captain, I being appointed interpreter, from my knowledge of Mahrattee; and we secured the best *shikarees*, huntsmen, possible. We rode to the village of Tamba, and on our arrival there learnt that our friend, the feline enemy, had killed a man the day before, and, while we were encamped, had carried off a poor woman during the night, within rifle-shot of our tent. This tigress was described to us as an enormous beast, with a long, lanky body, without a particle of hair on her back; and the natives were in such terror of her, that they offered up daily sacrifices to propitiate her.

We arrived at the place said to be haunted by this monster, and our beaters, of which we had a large number, being duly posted, as well as ourselves, by our captain, I found myself placed in one of the most tigerish-looking places I ever saw, with only my double-barrelled Westley Richards rifle to defend myself with and a spare gun carried by a native, who was in hiding behind a tree, and who would doubtless bolt when danger appeared!

As we advanced we beat the jungles in every direction for three or four days, with the additional noise of tom-toms and fireworks to drive her out; but though we came across her *pugs*, and even went into her lair, where we saw plenty of bones, human and animal, yet we never succeeded in catching a sight of this diabolically cunning brute. We attributed our want of success principally to the fears of the huntsmen and beaters that some serious accident might occur from the well-known ferocity of the tigress, and our being nearly all novices, and also to a superstitious dread or feeling that it was hopeless to destroy her, as she bore a charmed life. I am glad to add that this proved false, for some time later another party was more fortunate, and she was eventually killed, to the great joy and relief of the inhabitants.

We were beginning to despair of any sport, when we received *khuber* or news of a large bear in a ravine about ten miles off. We at once started off in pursuit, and after a hard day's work we had the satisfaction of killing her. She was said to be, by Elliot and the huntsmen, one of the largest they had ever seen, and it took sixteen men to carry her to our camp.

On another day, Elliot and I were posted on the edge of a dense jungle, and after waiting patiently for some time, were on the point of going away in disgust, when we suddenly espied two bears coming round the corner of a large rock about sixty yards from us. We fired simultaneously, wounding both of them. We then traced them by the blood, and eventually the larger one took refuge in a cave, where she was afterwards despatched, and the skin—a fine one—came into my possession.

A humorous scene occurred on this occasion, for when we were scrambling up the steep sides of the precipice, through dense jungle, in single file, and just as we were gaining the summit, the bear, enraged by the noise of our approach, suddenly rushed out to the mouth of the cave, uttering a tremendous growl. I, who happened to be in front, seeing that I could not possibly use my rifle, which I only grasped with one hand, while with the other I was clinging to a branch to support myself, instinctively jumped aside with much celerity, so as to allow our friend Bruin a free passage, not relishing the idea of a hug and rolling down the hill in her embrace; but in my energy I upset my companions, who were following close behind, like a pack of cards, to their great confusion and disgust. Fortunately, the bear, seeing nothing of us in the thick jungle, and being doubtless weakened by his wound, retreated into the cave again, and was soon after killed, as stated above.

On another occasion we received news that a tiger had killed a bullock, and the owner had run nearly all the way (eighteen miles) to inform us of this, begging us to come and kill the brute, as it was causing him much loss; and added that the tiger had been disturbed before making a meal of it, and would doubtless come during the night to do so. We at once got on our horses, reaching the spot before sunset, and set to work to rig up a *muchãn*, or temporary platform, made of branches in one of the large trees near where the carcass lay. Here, being well hidden, we took up our station, and, with our rifles across our knees, squatted *à la Turque,* waiting patiently for his lordship in silence. Hours passed—the darkness increased, and the awful stillness and gloom of the forest became oppressive. At length, when I was nearly asleep, though in a very cramped and uncomfortable position, I was roused by a gentle touch on the arm from my *shikaree,* and I then heard a rustling in the jungle, and saw the figure of the tiger, who uttered a short, deep cough, approaching his booty. The light of the moon, however, was so dim that we could not distinguish him clearly to have a good shot, and waited till he was helping himself to beef! But something seemed to disturb him or arouse his suspicions, for he suddenly bolted, and we never got a shot at him, to our huge disgust. This may have been due to our having, perhaps unwisely, caused the carcass to be moved some yards nearer to the tree where we were, as we thought it was too far off in the dim light to get a good shot at him. Our return to camp at midnight and by torchlight was very picturesque but not altogether pleasant, since, for aught we knew, the brute might now in his turn be stalking us; so we did not linger in our path. Thus ended our brief experience of tiger and bear hunting; and though we had comparatively indifferent sport (two bears and some deer, I think), we all enjoyed ourselves very much. The scenery of the valley of the Koncan, with its clear and sparkling stream of the Koinar winding through it, its banks clothed almost to the water's edge with splendid forest trees, is really grand, while the jungles abound with game, and the river affords good fishing.

Our leave of absence having nearly expired, we returned to Poona and duty again. Since writing the above, some years after, I find that poor Elliot, whose constitution was no doubt severely affected by his terrible encounter with the tiger, has joined *the great majority*, and that another of the party, the gallant young Newbury, a cornet in the lancers, was killed during the Mutiny when charging with his regiment a large body of the mutineers.

For some time there had been rumours afloat that there was every probability of our being involved in a war with Persia, as that Government, instigated by Russia, with whom we were then at war in the Crimea, had seized upon Herat, contrary to treaty. Herat is considered a point of great strategic importance, and in fact the key or gate of India. Having, therefore, a good deal of time at my disposal, I embraced the opportunity of studying the Persian language, believing that, owing to the fact of our proximity to Bombay, and of being the only rifle regiment of the Indian Army with its full complement of European officers—and being, moreover, commanded by a first-rate officer—there was every probability of our being sent to Persia; and so it turned out. The colloquial knowledge I acquired of that soft and beautiful language (like the Italian) proved of the greatest use to me and my brother officers, who often appealed to me to act as their interpreter.

On the 1st November 1856 war was formally declared against Persia, and we soon after learnt, to our delight, that we were to form the advance guard of the Persian Expeditionary Force, under command of General Stalker, C.B., and subsequently of General Sir James Outram, G.C.B.

CHAPTER 10

The Persian Campaign

Our regiment left Poona on 3rd November 1856, and duly reached the Khandalla Ghaut, our baggage being carried by elephants and camels. While *en route,* I paid a hasty visit to the celebrated Caves of Karlee, filled with huge, grotesque stone figures of Hindoo gods beautifully carved and said to be four thousand years old. They were well worth seeing.

On descending the Ghaut to Campoolee, we found a railway train awaiting us, and crossing the Tanna River, we soon arrived at Bombay, and encamped near the Borce Bandur. Our sipahees were much interested and delighted with this their first experience of railway travelling, the line having only recently been completed. During our short stay at Bombay we were inspected by the Commander-in-Chief, and on 13th November we embarked on board the steamer *Feroze* amid the hearty cheers and good wishes of our friends.

The Persian war being followed immediately by the great Indian Mutiny, was so eclipsed and dwarfed by the gigantic and alarming proportions of the latter, that sufficient importance, it is thought, has not been given to the former. Though of comparatively short duration, it was a very successful and brilliant campaign. This will not be wondered at when it is remembered that the command subsequently devolved on such distinguished generals as Outram, Havelock, and Jacob—all men of world-wide reputation.

Beyond, however, a partial account of the operations in Persia published by my gallant and lamented friend Captain Hunt of the 78th Highlanders, who did not arrive till after the fall of Bushire, and consequently was not an eye-witness of the earlier operations, I am not aware of any complete history of the campaign being in existence. Such being the case, and as I had the good fortune to belong to the advance guard of the expeditionary force, and was present throughout all the land operations—and, moreover, kept a journal of the same—I cannot perhaps do better than give such extracts from it as may prove of interest to the reader.

13th November 1856.—Early this morning, the steam frigate *Feroze,* with the Headquarters of my regiment on board, steamed out of Bombay harbour for Bushire, having in tow two transports conveying the Poona Horse and sappers and miners.

19th November.—Off Cape Rask and opposite Kohee Moobarak (the Blessed Mountain), the first Persian land—high, rocky, mountainous shore—entered the Persian Gulf, the coast of Arabia in sight. Passed the islands of Kishm and Ormuz, on which last there is a fort built by the Portuguese, but now belonging to the Imaum of Muscat. We dropped anchor at Bundur Abbas. This fine harbour is to be the general rendezvous of our fleet and transports, being from its size and depth of water capable of holding all our expeditionary ships and transports with ease. It has lately come much to the front from the fact that Russia is intriguing to possess it or lease it. Our Government have, however, distinctly intimated to Persia that this would not be permitted, as it would be a standing menace to India; for this harbour could be enlarged, and with the adjoining islands Kishm and Ormuz be made a second Sebastopol, which would be within about a week's steam of Bombay.

21st November.—The steam frigate *Assaye* arrived here with General Stalker, C.B., commanding the Persian Field

Force, and Commodore Sir H. Leeke the Naval Squadron—also several transports with troops on board, so that altogether there was a creditable force here.

27th.—Leaving Bundur Abbas, we passed the rocky isles of Larak and Polior and the town of Bassadore, coasting nearly the whole way, and on the afternoon of the 29th November we reached Bushire, and anchored in the roadstead opposite the town, eight miles off.

Viewed from the sea-board, Bushire has rather an imposing appearance. It is defended by a high wall and bastions, and is situated on a narrow neck or spit of land washed on two faces by the sea and a swampy creek.

The Resident or Political Agent here, Captain Felix Jones, and his suite came on board the *Feroze* the following morning, and we learnt from him that there was every prospect of our soon having some fighting" with our Persian friends, which elated us all very much.

1st December.—Captain Taylor, assistant to the Honourable Mr. Murray, Ambassador at the Persian Court, arrived from Bagdad bearing important despatches from the Home Government regarding Persian affairs.

3rd December.—Warlike preparations are to be commenced at once, and we open the campaign by the formal occupation of the island of Karack, some thirty miles from Bushire, at the head of the Persian Gulf, which it commands, and whence, moreover, the principal or best supply of water is obtained, Bushire being deficient in that respect.

We left the same afternoon for that destination in the *Feroze* with our Colonel Brigadier Honner and his staff, and also Captain Desbrowe, the Assistant Political Agent, and reached it the same evening. Next morning the troops disembarked, and the island was formally taken possession of in the name of Her Majesty, under a salute of twenty-one guns, and the Union Jack was hoisted on the principal buildings. The troops presenting arms were formed into three sides of a hollow square, the remaining side being occupied by the inhabitants, mostly fishermen; while a proclamation was read in Persian and English by the Political Officer, annexing the island to the British dominions. A strong company of the Belooch Battalion under a European officer was left to garrison the place, and a commissariat officer and staff.

It having been decided by the authorities that the point of descent on the coast should be at Huleelah Bay, about thirteen miles south of Bushire, the whole fleet left on the morning of the 6th, and arrived there the same afternoon.

On the following morning, which happened to be Sunday, the troops landed under cover of the gunboats, which shelled the village, and drove out the enemy's scouts, who were seen galloping off towards Bushire.

In landing, we had to wade up to our waists, and had we then encountered any serious resistance, it would have gone hard with us. Thus was our first footing on Persian soil made good. In the afternoon I was sent in command of a hundred men to take possession of some wells about two miles off, in the vicinity of a small village. Seeing some of the enemy's horsemen hovering about, I directed a native officer with a strong patrol to reconnoitre the ground in front, in the performance of which duty they were fired upon, and returned the compliment; and thus the first shots of this campaign were exchanged with my detachment.

Observing that these horsemen were becoming more numerous and bold, I deemed it advisable to get my small detachment under the best cover available, which happened to be a ditch or trench adjoining the wells, wherein I posted my men, and awaited results ; but though they made sundry feints of charging, they never did so.

In the evening the force came up and bivouacked a little in advance of my post, and the following day the whole of the troops had landed and rejoined us.

As we officers had only some biscuits and salt beef in our haversacks, I was very glad to partake of a capital stew of fowl, concocted by my friend Lieutenant Holland of the Quarter-Master General's Department in his *Soyer's patent stove.*

On the following morning (9th), the force marched on the village of Charbagh, where the advance guard had an engagement with the enemy, and suffered some loss. The first object that met our sight was the body of one of our unfortunate camp-followers, who had been decapitated.

Soon after we arrived before the fort of Reshire, which was garrisoned by about two thousand Arabs of the Tengistooni tribe, who bore the character of being a very martial race, which their determined resistance in the severe action that now took place did not belie. This fort, situated near the seaside, though not a large one, had thick mud walls, with bastions at the angles, and broad ramparts, lined with deep pits, where the enemy lay concealed; and it was further strengthened by a deep, dry moat around it. To attack this our force numbered about three thousand men, and consisted of a troop of horse artillery and a field battery, some squadrons of the 3rd Bombay Cavalry and Poona Horse, H.M.'s 64th Foot, 2nd Bombay European Light Infantry, 20th Regiment Native Infantry, the Belooch Battalion, and the 4th Rifles, the last named being on the extreme left and thrown out into skirmishing order, covering our left flank.

As our little army advanced in imposing battle array, covered by a line of skirmishers with their supports and reserves, and our flanks protected by artillery and cavalry, we were met by a bold and determined front, and soon found ourselves in the midst of a heavy and continuous fire, which we returned with interest. The enemy were principally armed with long match-locks of a superior kind, many of them having flint-locks of English manufacture, which carried an immense distance and did considerable execution. While we were steadily advancing, our men were much annoyed by a small mosque on our left flank, whence I was directed by a staff officer to dislodge them, which was effected in gallant style by my company. My subaltern, Lieutenant Sangster, particularly distinguished himself on this occasion, charging with the bayonet.

At length, after a severe struggle which lasted several hours, we gained possession of this fort, but not without heavy loss, our casualties numbering about fifty, including several officers. Among the number killed were Brigadier Stopford, C. B., and Colonel Malet, commanding the cavalry, both excellent officers. The latter was basely shot by a wretch whose life he only a few minutes before had spared.

One officer received no less than eight wounds, and for his gallantry subsequently received the Victoria Cross.

The loss of the enemy was very great, and we also captured several horses, one of which came into my possession, and was called by me Tengistooni, in remembrance of our fight with that warlike Arab tribe. The fort itself was destroyed by us.

Early next morning the funeral of the officers and men killed took place, the Rev. W. Watson, the Chaplain, officiating. Immediately after the force advanced on Bushire, and arriving there about noon, called upon the town authorities to surrender, the Indian Navy having pounded and shelled the town for some hours, to which we also added a few gentle reminders in the way of shells, and which were feebly responded to. At length, utterly disheartened and dismayed, they struck their flag and surrendered unconditionally, and some fifteen hundred soldiers issued out of the main gate, and laid down their arms in front of our little army drawn up in line. The Governor, Duriya Beg, was made a prisoner of war, and afterwards sent to Bombay. The soldiers who had laid down their arms were permitted to go unmolested, an act of grace due mainly to their having allowed a European soldier whom they had taken prisoner to return to camp in safety.

The following night, to oblige a brother officer, who wished to visit his brother, who had been wounded and conveyed on board ship, I went in his place on outlying picket duty, and my subaltern and myself had the felicity of being kept under arms, without cover, for nearly *thirty* hours before we were relieved.

On the 13th, the tents, baggage, etc., of the force having been landed, the camp was pitched about a mile from the town and close to the seashore, and with the shipping in the offing had a cheerful appearance. The day following being Sunday, divine service was performed in the open air by our Chaplain, the Holy Communion administered, of which I with others partook, I trust, with a thankful heart for being spared through the dangers we had encountered.

One day, in company with some brother officers, we made an excursion into the town of Bushire, the population of which consists mainly of Persians, Arabs, Jews, and Armenians. The last named were most intelligent. They belonged to the Greek Church, and were chiefly engaged in commercial pursuits. The streets are narrow and not very clean, but our energetic Bazaar Master will soon improve matters. The Residency and the house of Mr. Malcum, an Armenian merchant and a British subject, are the best in the town, and there is also a good covered-in bazaar.

Our camp is entrenched by a trench about three feet deep and six feet in breadth, with earth thrown up as a parapet, and faces the town, stretching across to the isthmus, and we have a cavalry picket a few miles in front, by way of outpost and to prevent any surprise. Of the enemy we have seen nothing since the capture of Bushire, though there is a rumour that they are collecting in force between this and Shiraz, with the object of attacking us, probably at night, their favourite mode of warfare.

It behoves us therefore to be on the *qui vive,* and to use all precautions towards strengthening our position. We have now sufficient leisure to enjoy a sea-bath and an occasional visit to our naval friends. I have also resumed my study of the Persian language with an intelligent native, who speaks English well and professes to be a Christian, but I have doubts about him; and I learn that Colonel Ballard of the Intelligence Department is hunting up a spy in camp, and I strongly suspect it is my friend the *moonshee*, who suddenly disappeared!

3rd January 1857.—This morning a reconnoitring party consisting of three hundred cavalry and four guns under command of Colonel Tapp which had been sent out on the Shiraz road to destroy a quantity of powder, ammunition, grain, etc., at a depot belonging to the enemy some fifteen miles off, returned after having successfully performed their duty, and received the thanks of the general commanding.

The small schooner *Euphrates* armed with heavy guns has been brought a good way up the creek to protect our right flank, and will doubtless do us good service in case an attack is threatened. On the 8th, the Hon. Mr. Murray, the Ambassador at the Persian Court, arrived with his suite from Bagdad, which was announced with the usual salute, and took up his quarters at the Residency. The following day the whole force marched out to Reshire by way of a demonstration, as well as for the sake of exercise, to give confidence to the townspeople.

We had several of these route-marching parades to keep the men in good marching trim. On one of these occasions, commanded by our Brigadier, the whole division returned homewards in the order of battle, my regiment being thrown out into skirmishing order, with a light field battery at each flank. In a second line as our right support was the 64th Regiment drawn up in quarter-distance column, while the left support was formed by the 20th Regiment Native Infantry, and sappers in similar formation. In the third line was the 2nd Europeans and Belooch Battalion, the reserve consisting of the cavalry—altogether a most imposing array.

About this period occurred the sad and lamented death of General Stalker, which cast a gloom over us; but shortly after we were cheered by the arrival of General Sir James Outram, K.C.B., to take the chief command, and he brought with him on the 27th January a welcome addition to our troops, including our old Poona friends the gallant 78th Highlanders, who caused much sensation among the Persians. The 26th Regiment Native Infantry and others also arrived, and we had a goodly array.

CHAPTER 11

The Persian Campaign
—Continued

EXPEDITION TO BORĀZJOON

The arrival of our Indian Bayard, General Sir James Outram, G.C.B., with reinforcements, as mentioned in the last
chapter, was welcomed by us all with enthusiasm. The Highlanders, in their kilts and with their bagpipes playing, caused
much astonishment among the natives. Soon signs of energy
and activity were visible, which took shape in the expedition to Borāzjoon, some fifty miles off, where the enemy had
collected a vast quantity of supplies, ammunition, troops, and
guns, with the object of sweeping down on "the accursed
Feringhees," and driving us into the sea! General Outram,
who was in immediate command, proposed to anticipate this
daring little scheme, and very quietly, and without any fuss,
directed that the troops should have plenty of route-marching
exercise to keep them in good condition ; and with this object
they were frequently marched out to Charkota, some dozen
miles off, which was our extreme cavalry outlying picket.

The enemy, who by their spies were well acquainted with
our movements, attributed this frequent marching and coun-
ter-marching back to camp again to our fear and dread of
attacking them, and were thus thrown off their guard, as the
General hoped to surprise them. In the meanwhile, silently

but promptly arrangements were made for a *dour*, or forced march, on the enemy: provisions of cooked beef and biscuits for the Europeans, and *chapaties*, or flour cakes, for the sipahees—to be carried by themselves, no tents or commissariat beyond some spare ammunition, etc.

The troops comprising this expedition consisted of the 64th Foot, 78th Highlanders, 2nd Bombay European Light Infantry, 4th Rifles, 20th and 26th Bombay Regiments Native Infantry, and 2nd Belooch Battalion, one troop of horse artillery, and two batteries of field artillery, 3rd Bombay Light Cavalry and Poona Horse—altogether, about three thousand European and native troops.

It was a bold and dashing expedition, but our General was fully equal to the occasion, as the result proved.

The whole of the Persian Expeditionary Force, with all the reinforcements, had now arrived, and amounted to a *Corps d'Armée* of ten thousand; so that, besides our expedition to Borãzjoon, there were some seven thousand men in reserve at Bushire and its neighbourhood to protect us against all risks.

Accordingly, all requisite arrangements having thus been very quietly made, we on the afternoon of the 3rd February 1857, started on our dash across country to anticipate the enemy's intention of attacking us, and if possible to surprise them.

We marched all night over heavy sand and swampy ground, halting a few hours at Charkota, our outlying outpost. Resuming our march amid clouds of sand blowing right in our teeth, we about 10 p.m. bivouacked for the night on a sandy plain, having altogether made a forced march of some forty miles. The men were much knocked up by it, and during the night, to add to our troubles, a tremendous thunder-storm broke upon us, accompanied by hail and a piercingly cold wind. We were drenched to the skin, as we had no cover beyond our cloaks. It was altogether most trying, and one of our poor Highlanders died during the night from extreme exhaustion and exposure combined.

Early the following morning we resumed our march on Borãzjoon, taking the precaution to discharge and reload our arms after the downpour of rain we had experienced.

As we sighted the enemy's camp, our cavalry and horse artillery advanced to the front, and three companies of my regiment (the Rifles) under my command were thrown out into skirmishing order as an advance guard. Shots were exchanged with some of the enemy's cavalry with but little damage, though our Colonel had a narrow escape, a ball having passed through his clothes and lodged in the tree of his saddle. As we approached their entrenchment, the enemy, to our mortification, retreated rapidly to the hills, carrying off some of their guns, while we at once took possession of the entrenched camp; and a large quantity of grain, rice, flour, ammunition, etc., fell into our hands, as well as some guns, which we spiked, being unable to carry them off for want of carriage.

The town of Borãzjoon was within a mile of camp, and we were allowed to go there in armed bodies; for, though not molested, the looks and bearing of the inhabitants were not inviting, and it was deemed necessary to make a prisoner of the Governor.

So far our expedition had been quite successful, for, in capturing their camp and mounting eighteen guns with comparatively little loss, we had also got possession of large quantities of stores, disabled many guns, and destroyed an enormous quantity of ammunition and powder, exploded by means of Jacob's shells, by Lieutenants Gibbard and Hassard, after our leaving the camp, at a distance of nearly five hundred yards, causing tremendous concussion and throwing down these officers by the shock.

After our men had rested and been refreshed, we on the evening of the 7th resumed our return march, little dreaming of what was in store for us!

The 4th Rifles (my regiment) formed the rearguard, supported by two horse artillery guns and a squadron of native

cavalry, which force was commanded by our Colonel, Brigadier Honner, a first-rate officer. I was directed, with the two
leading companies, to extend the files and keep in touch as
much as possible with the main body, who were with the
chief and his staff in advance.

This was no easy task, as our progress was of necessity
slower than the rest of the troops, for we were hampered by
the captured grain-wagons, of which we had charge; and I
had just reported to the Brigadier that our distance from the
main body and rest of the force was increasing rapidly, and
that I had extended my men to the utmost limit, when I was
directed to push on as fast as we could, as no danger was then
apprehended.

Night fell: it was pitch dark, and about midnight the whole
heavens seemed lighted up, and our devoted rear-guard was
enveloped in a circle of fire! The enemy, moreover, suddenly appeared all around us, screaming and yelling like fiends,
blowing trumpets and bugles furiously, their horsemen galloping about in a frantic manner, and causing as much noise
and confusion as possible, evidently with the object of creating a panic among us. Fortunately, our Brigadier was a soldier
of nerve and great presence of mind, and by his able handling
of the troops and the remarkable steadiness of the men (who
had perfect confidence in him), the enemy were repulsed, and
we regained the main body, which had halted, without even
losing any of our baggage.

For our steadiness in the face of a large force of the enemy, when taken at every disadvantage, we were subsequently
highly commended by the General; and the Brigadier, for this
and other services in the campaign, received the well-merited
honour of the Companionship of the Bath.

While this affair lasted my subaltern and I were galloping
backwards and forwards, looking after our men, when, during the sudden flash of a gun in the darkness, I espied at some
distance off—about three hundred yards—a riderless charger

standing like a graven image beside a prostrate, motionless figure on the ground. I drew Lieutenant Sangster's attention to the same, and we at once galloped up to see who it was.

"Good God! it is the General!" exclaimed my companion.

We were horror-struck, and thought at first that he was killed.

"I'm not wounded, but fell from my horse when galloping back on hearing the attack on the rearguard!" said a feeble voice, to our relief.

We gave Sir James some brandy, which revived him, as he seemed quite stunned and shaken, and I directed Sangster to report the matter at once to the Brigadier, and to procure a *doolie*, or litter, without delay, which he did; and he was eventually handed over to his Staff, who had been in vain searching for him everywhere, having lost him in the darkness.

It was a narrow escape, for we were in a critical position, and were being fired into by the enemy, who surrounded us. Had they found the General, what a great prize it would have been for them!

Our troubles, however, on this eventful night were far from being over, for the whole force being now formed into an immense hollow square, with the captured stores and baggage in the centre, the enemy, who had got our range nicely, kept pounding us for some hours.

We at first returned their fire, but subsequently we received orders to "cease firing"; and the enemy then thinking we had changed our position, ceased firing also, which was a great relief to us, as we were thus able to snatch a little fitful sleep after the fatigues and anxieties we had undergone.

Sangster and I, however, took the precaution of holding each other's hands, in case a change of movement might occur during our nap, and we should be left behind.

We all waited anxiously for daylight, that we might read the Persian Army a lesson after their favourite Parthian mode of attack, though fearing that they would deem "discretion the better part of valour"; but, to our great satisfaction, on the morning of the memorable 8th February 1857 we found the enemy drawn up in strong array offering us battle, which we speedily accepted. The Persians were drawn up in line in a good position, with two hillocks in front of their centre mounting guns, and rising ground covering their flanks. They numbered about eight thousand men, including some two thousand cavalry, and were commanded by Soojah-ool-Moolk, one of their best officers.

Altogether, they looked an imposing force with their tall felt or lambskin hats like our guardsmen.

Our troops numbered about three thousand of all arms.

We speedily deployed, and were drawn up in two lines, consisting of the 78th Highlanders with some sappers and miners on the right, then the 26th Regiment Native Infantry, the 2nd European Light Infantry, and the 4th Bombay Rifles on the extreme left. The second line was composed of the 64th Foot, the 20th Regiment Native Infantry, and the Belooch Battalion on the left, while the cavalry and horse artillery were principally posted on the right front.

The action commenced by a brisk cannonade on both sides, under cover of which our troops advanced rapidly and steadily to the front; and though several casualties occurred during this period, the line was unbroken, while our skirmishers covering our flanks and rear, aided by some cavalry, protected the baggage and kept the enemy at bay in that quarter. As we advanced closer the cannonading became furious, and our fine artillery made beautiful practice, while our 3rd Bombay Native Cavalry executed a most brilliant charge under command of Major Forbes, actually breaking through a Persian square, and committing great slaughter among them. Lieutenant Moore, the Adjutant of this regiment, with daring Irish pluck actually jumped his horse into the square, thus making an opening for his troopers. He had a wonderful escape, his horse being killed, and he himself was rescued by a brother officer, Lieutenant Malcolmson, and both of them justly received the Victoria Cross.

A spirited sketch of this dashing charge appeared subsequently in the *Illustrated London News.*

The enemy after this, seeing our line advancing in unbroken array, lost heart, broke, and fled in all directions, leaving several guns in our possession.

Their cavalry behaved very ill, for on a fortunate shot from an Enfield rifle, by Lieutenant Gillespie of the 2nd Europeans, at about eight hundred yards, killing their leader who was prancing about in a defiant manner *à la Goliath,* they vanished out of sight!

Thus ended the battle of Khooshàb (Sweet Water), so called from the village of that name, which resulted in the total defeat of the Persian Army.

The General, unfortunately, owing to his serious accident (though present on the field), was unable to take any active part in this action, which, however, was skilfully conducted by his able chief of the staff—Colonel, afterwards Sir Edward, Lugard. Our casualties were about eighty, and among them we had to deplore the loss of my lamented friend Lieutenant Frankland of the 2nd European Light Infantry—a most promising officer.

Upwards of seven hundred of the enemy lay dead on the field, and their wounded were carried away by their friends.

Our return march to Bushire on the 10th February was a severe and trying one owing to the swampy nature of the ground and the heavy rain, but we were rewarded for all our trials and fatigue by receiving the hearty cheers and congratulations of our comrades.

A most complimentary and appreciatory Field Force Order, dated 10th February 1857, was issued by General Outram, in which he gave a graphic account of this very successful expedition: the capture of the enemy's entrenched camp, the gallant repulse of the night attack on the rear-guard, and the decisive battle of Khooshàb, and the General concluded—

This result is most satisfactory, and .will, the Lieutenant-General trusts, have a very beneficial effect on the
future operations in Persia. The Lieutenant-General
therefore feels that he cannot too strongly express his
obligations to the officers and men of all arms for the
almost incredible exertions they have undergone and
the gallantry they have displayed on the occasion.
By Command.
(Signed) *E. Lugard*
Colonel
Chief of the Staff

CHAPTER 12

The Persian Campaign —Concluded

The day following our arrival at Bushire the funeral of Lieutenant Frankland and those who had fallen in the action of the 8th February took place, and nearly all the officers of the force attended.

Owing to the hardships, cold, and exposure we had lately endured, there was much sickness, especially among the native troops. My regiment had almost two hundred in hospital, and other regiments suffered in nearly equal proportions.

About this period General Havelock and his staff arrived, bringing some reinforcements, and my regiment was placed in his division. I remember well our being reviewed by this distinguished officer, who expressed himself well satisfied with us. He was a thin, slightly built, but wiry-looking man, with piercing grey eyes and somewhat stern appearance, while his well-known character as a strict disciplinarian was amply borne out by the firmness and decision visible in his countenance.

As he walked down the ranks with folded arms, narrowly inspecting us, he caught a man looking at him instead of to his front, and exclaimed, "Why, this man is inspecting *me,* and I came to inspect *him!*"

Though always highly thought of, little did we then realise

that his name would soon become famous throughout the Empire!

The arrival of a copy of the official *Teheran Government Gazette* in camp (which was translated by our Persian interpreter, Captain Rigby) caused us much amusement, for referring to our invasion of Persia as "unprovoked," and denouncing out expedition to Borãzjoon, it wound up by saying that "The British had been defeated, and driven back with great slaughter!" As a specimen of plausible fiction, so characteristic of Persian duplicity and lying, it was grand! And we heard afterwards that they received a medal for the victory!

It having been decided by the authorities that another expedition should shortly be despatched to attack the fortified town of Mohammarah, about three days' sail hence, and situated at the confluence of the Shãt-el-Arab and Karoon rivers, where a large force was being assembled under the *Shahzada* (one of the Royal Princes), a combined naval and military force was speedily prepared for that purpose, under the immediate command of Sir James Outram.

My regiment was to have formed part of this expedition, but at the last moment this was countermanded in favour of the 23rd Bombay Light Infantry (Outram's own regiment), which arrived just in time, and it was deemed only fair that they should have their chance of seeing service.

In the meanwhile, as this expedition would considerably reduce the strength of the garrison at Bushire, active preparations were made by the engineers and sappers to erect five strong redoubts, armed with heavy guns and manned by native troops, to defend our entrenchment and camp. It was deemed probable that the enemy, being apprised of the reduction of our force, would, according to their favourite tactics, attempt a night attack.

Large fatigue parties of our sipahees were therefore employed daily in carrying to the appointed place *fascines* made by the sappers from branches of trees, etc. On one of these occasions, when in command of a party, one of my men—a Hindoo of high caste—demurred to doing this, saying it was against his caste, and brought a *coolie* to do his work. I, however, objected to allow his duty being done by deputy, and pointed out that carrying sticks had nothing to do with his caste, for he used the self-same materials to cook his meals with, and sternly ordered him to obey, which he did very reluctantly, for I threatened otherwise to make him a prisoner, and give him a court-martial. I have no doubt that had I not thus acted, the other men even of less high caste than himself would have refused too!

A very different case occurred on the steamer in which the headquarters of my regiment came here, for owing to the ignorance and stupidity of the sailors, a bullock was killed on deck, near where the men were, and close to the open butts where their drinking water was. This was a gross and wanton outrage to the religious feelings of the many Hindoos who were there, as the cow is a sacred animal with them, and they also thought that being in such close proximity to their drinking water it would be defiled; as I was the interpreter, they came up to me in an excited but respectful manner, and protested against this, which I reported to the commanding officer, who was very angry with the ship authorities, and ordered that the animal should be removed at once. He also directed that in future the cattle should be killed between decks, out of sight of the men. The drinking water was changed, and all was quiet again. These very men fought splendidly against their countrymen and co-religionists during the great Mutiny, and we had not a single case of desertion!

The troops having left for Mohammarah, I was soon after placed in command of one of these redoubts with some gunners, under a young artillery officer, to work the guns, and a company of the Belooch Battalion. These men are fine, martial, wild-looking fellows, and might be aptly styled the *Zouaves* of our Indian Army, for they also, like those gentry,

98

have very elastic notions of *meum* and *tuum*. An instance of this occurred during my charge, for one day a villager came to me and complained bitterly that a favourite goat of his had been stolen by my men, who all innocently disclaimed all knowledge of the same. I inquired what colour it was, and the owner said it was a fine black goat; I directed a search to be made among the men's kits, and there sure enough the black skin was found! The men were punished and made to pay the owner the value of his goat.

We in command of the redoubts received strict injunctions to keep a sharp lookout against any attack, especially at night, and to post guards and sentries to be regularly relieved, and we were told that a signal gun would be fired by way of a warning in the event of the enemy's approach. All was quiet till one night we heard the signal gun, and immediately the men sprang to their arms with lighted fusees, ready for action. No attack, however, was made, and I think this was done more to test our being on the *qui vive,* which proved satisfactory.

The combined naval and military attack on Mohammarah took place on the morning of the 26th March by a severe bombardment, the first shell falling right into the enemy's works, and killing many. The Persians replied with spirit, and stood to their guns manfully for some hours; but eventually the fire slackened, when our troops, led by the Highlanders and 64th Foot, landed and captured the entrenched camp, and after some resistance the enemy fled, with the *Shahzada*, or royal prince, at their head.

The pursuit was continued by the Scinde Horse, and also by a small armed steamer, up the Karoon River to Ahwaz, and large quantities of stores, ammunition, etc., were captured or destroyed ; and some eighteen brass guns, including a handsome 12-pounder, a present from the late Emperor of Russia, came into our possession.

In this expedition great credit was clue to the *Indian Navy* for the gallant manner in which they brought their vessels into action, and also for their crushing and most effective bombardment; many of them were hulled by round shot, one being struck eight times.

Our troops took possession of the town of Mohammarah, and this last defeat coming so soon after the capture of fort of Reshire, the surrender of the important town of Bushire, the successful expedition to Borãzjoon, and the decisive battle of Khooshàb, brought to his senses the Shah of Persia, who impiously arrogates to himself the title of "The King of Kings." His Majesty soon after cried *Peccavi* and sued for peace, conceded *all* the British demands, including the important one of renouncing all pretensions to interfere in the affairs of Herat (The Gate of India) or any portion of Afghan territory, Persia being merely a tool of Russia. Thus closed the Persian war ; for General Outram, when issuing his last Field Force Order, highly eulogising his troops, informed them that it was at an end, as peace had been proclaimed. He thanked them warmly for their services, and bade them farewell. As regards our General himself in this brilliant campaign, no words could more fitly or justly apply to him than those used by Caesar, so pithily announcing his victories to the Roman Senate, *"Veni, vidi, vici!"*

I once again saw this distinguished officer, of whom the Indian Army is justly proud; and his still greater and more splendid services in the great Mutiny, during the relief of Lucknow and its most illustrious garrison, and his chivalrous conduct to General Havelock in yielding to him the supreme command, though his junior, may well entitle him to be styled *The Bayard of the Indian Army* (as Sir C. Napier called him), *"sans peur et sans reproche."*

Some years after his lamented death, when travelling in Scotland, I met his son, Sir Francis, to whom I mentioned various details and particulars of his father's severe fall from his horse during the night attack on the rearguard, mentioned in the last chapter, and which he had never fully heard before. He was so much interested that he introduced me to his mother, the Dowager Lady Outram, who was equally interested, and expressed her obligations to me for his timely rescue.

À *propos* of the Shah of Persia, how little could I or anyone have dreamt that, several years after, I should have seen his successor (or his son) to the throne of King Darius, in London, at the Albert Hall, arm in arm with our present Queen, and the honoured guest of our nation! This, I believe, is the first instance of a strictly Oriental monarch being received on intimate terms at the British Court.

It was fortunate for the interests of India and our empire that this campaign was brought to so speedy a conclusion, for about this time very serious news reached us of the outbreak of mutiny in the Bengal Army, which spread and grew to such great proportions. This caused the speedy departure of our European regiments, the 64th Foot and the 78th Highlanders, for India, both of which regiments arrived in the nick of time, and performed splendid services at Lucknow and Cawnpore.

Our force was further reduced under the command of General John Jacob, C.B., another distinguished Indian officer, the organiser and commander of the celebrated *Jacob's Scinde Horse*, serving on the north-west frontier of India, where I had the honour of meeting him.

My regiment was now quartered in the town of Bushire, which we were very glad of, as we got comfortable quarters in the houses there, and I was fortunate enough to secure a double-storeyed one to share with a brother-officer, which had a flat roof, where we slept in more comfort, enjoying the cold sea-breezes.

The town of Bushire was much indebted to Captain Rigby, our energetic bazaar-master, for the sanitary arrangements he carried out in cleansing and purifying it, establishing an excellent bazaar with ample and good provisions, organising a small body of police to keep order there, and generally beautifying and improving the town, including a nice promenade on the sea front.

Captain Felix Jones, of the Indian Navy, was the Political Agent, whose hospitality I frequently enjoyed in his fine residence, and it was delightful after dinner to smoke a cigar with him on the terraced fiat roof.

He married an Armenian lady, who was absent at this time, but whom I subsequently met at Norwood with her charming daughters. He introduced me to the leading Armenian merchant there, Mr. Malcum, and his nice family of daughters, with whom I became very friendly, and improved my knowledge of Persian by conversation with them, and also studying the

Bagh-o-buhar and *Gulistan,* two famous Persian books. My brother-officers jealously envied me, as they were not able to speak Persian. The family were Christians belonging to the Greek Church, and were British subjects.

Leave being now thrown open to officers, I, in company with a brother-officer, obtained six weeks' leave from General Jacob, to proceed to Bagdad, and visit the ruins of Babylon, which I, being fond of travel, was most desirous to see. Accordingly, about the end of May we left Bushire, and proceeded to Bagdad.

Chapter 13

India and the Bheel Campaign

We returned from our interesting trip to Babylon in time for muster parade on the 1st July, and heard still further alarming accounts of the spread of the great Indian Mutiny.

The month of July passed quietly away at Bushire, and it was not so hot as we anticipated.

During our absence an entertainment had been given to the *aide-de-camp* of the Persian commander-in-chief, who, after the Treaty of Peace had been concluded, had come to Bushire to pay his respects to our chief, Sir James Outram. The mess tent was brilliantly illuminated with numerous Persian lamps, the band was in attendance, and there were present officers in uniform, together with numerous guests invited in honour of the occasion. Soon after, Colonel Trevelyan and Captain Desbrowe, the Assistant Political Agent, returned the visit, and were hospitably received by the *Cheekee-Bashee*, or Persian Governor of Borãzjoon.

The engrossing topic of conversation with us was of course the great Mutiny, and it was with deep anxiety and eagerness that we watched the progress of events, our attention being principally fixed on Delhi, where the rebels were in great force with powerful artillery. The British force besieging it was far too weak at this time to accomplish so gigantic a task as of capturing it, and had already suffered terribly from the fearful heat, cholera, and war casualties. Reinforcements, however, were expected as well as a siege train from the Punjáb, and it was hoped that we should soon be able to assume the offensive. Truly an awful retribution awaited these misguided wretches, who had been guilty of such terrible atrocities, for Nemesis was at hand!

I spoke freely and openly to our native officers, considering it to be the wisest course and best policy, for they heard the wildest rumours in the bazaar, as they themselves told me, and seemed perfectly satisfied when I told them the real state of affairs. I took care, however, to point out to them the wretched infatuation of the rebels, and that though they were at present in possession of Delhi, which they had seized by treachery, yet gradually our troops were closing round them, and reinforcements arriving, while they were quarrelling among themselves, all wishing to be leaders, etc.

Some of my brother-officers did not approve of this, wishing rather to treat them in a distant manner, as though they were objects of suspicion, and thereby utterly estranging them. But as I had closely studied the native character, and associated much with them, I felt persuaded that the plan I adopted was the best to pursue under the circumstances. There was a natural anxiety lest this infection should spread to our Presidency (Bombay), but although we had many Bengal Sipahees in our ranks, and it could scarcely be expected that some isolated cases of mutiny and disaffection would not arise, yet owing to our more rigid discipline and other causes, I am proud to say that our army was sound and loyal, as subsequent events amply proved. Many of our regiments, mine among the number, fought against their countrymen and co-religionists in this mutiny. The Madras Army also was staunch, though there were some isolated cases of disaffection.

I was glad to renew my acquaintance with my fair Armenian friends, who always received me with the kind words "Khoosh Amudeed" (Welcome). The girls were dressed picturesquely in semi-Oriental style, wearing small turbans surmounted by coquettish-looking red caps with tassels, and reminded me of pictures of Byron's Maid of Athens.

In thus combining pleasure with instruction I improved my knowledge of Persian, but my brother-officers being envious of this, I one day received a letter purporting to be from the father, asking my intentions! Of course it was a hoax, which I quickly discovered.

The news of our speedy return to India much rejoiced us, especially as the weather was becoming oppressively hot. At night we could only get sleep on the flat roof of the house under a *chuppur*, or thatched awning, to protect us from the heavy dews.

The news from India continued very bad, Delhi being still in the hands of the mutineers, with Lucknow and Cawnpore closely besieged. We, however, were glad to learn that the traitors had been severely handled at Mhow by Hungerford's battery of European artillery, and that our gallant Bombay Lancers had proved themselves staunch at Neemuch by charging the miscreants and saving the lives of the European residents and officers at that station, whom they escorted to a place of safety. On this occasion a gallant young officer, named Newbury, a friend of mine, was killed in the charge.

The time of our departure from Persian soil was now at hand. After a farewell review of my regiment by General Jacob, C.B., in which he highly complimented us, and after bidding good-bye to many friends, we embarked on the 15th August, under command of Major Manson.

In closing my account of this campaign, I may mention that my Indian regiment, now called H.M. Wellesley Rifles, from having served under the great Duke at the siege of Seringapatam, was the first to land on Persian soil and exchange shots with the enemy, and the last but one to leave after the close of the war.

We sailed in the fine ship *Haddington* (while our Colonel as Brigadier was left in command of the rest of the troops there), which in the course of a week was becalmed off Muscat.

The heat here was terrible, it being one of the hottest places in the world; high, barren, precipitous-hills surrounded the town, which was commanded by a castle on a rock. Viewed from the sea, Muscat has an imposing appearance.

Soon after leaving the place one of my brother-officers died of liver complaint, to our great regret, and was consigned to the deep, the captain reading the burial service.

Not long after leaving Muscat we encountered a stiff gale, which split our maintop-sail; but eventually, on the 1st September, the pilot came on board, and took us into the inner harbour of Bombay. On arrival, we learnt that Delhi, Cawnpore, and Lucknow were still in the hands of the rebels, and our prospects were consequently not cheering.

On the following morning we landed, and encamped on the esplanade. We found the European community somewhat uneasy; but all passed off quietly.

On the 7th we left for Poona, where we duly arrived, and were warmly greeted by our numerous friends. All of us were glad to get back to our old quarters again.

A few days after our arrival at Poona, tidings reached us of the awful and treacherous massacre of helpless women and children at Cawnpore by that fiend Nana Sahib; but the hour of stern retribution was at hand. Further reinforcements had arrived from England, and on the 25th September we learnt by telegraph the glorious news of the "Fall of Delhi," on the 18th of that month; but, alas! our loss was terrible, and among the number was the noble-hearted Nicholson, who led the storming party. Soon after, we heard that the wretched old puppet, the King of Delhi, had been deposed, and that his guilty sons, who had taken an active part in the butchery previous to the siege, had paid the penalty with their lives, at the hands of Major Hodson, the daring and splendid cavalry officer.

About the middle of October we also rejoiced to learn the glorious news of the first relief of Lucknow by Outram and Havelock, and their gallant band of heroes—who were subsequently reinforced by Sir Colin Campbell, afterwards Lord Clyde.

Our own stay in quiet quarters was of brief duration, for news arrived that the *Bheels*—a wild mountain tribe in the Khandeish and Nuggur districts—had broken out in insurrection, and were plundering and laying waste the country. A strong police force under Captain Henry had in the first instance been sent out (with whom was an officer of my regiment, Lieutenant Graham, who was wounded), but no satisfactory results were obtained. Therefore the Government decided on despatching a field force into the disturbed districts, of which a detachment of my regiment under Captain Langston formed part. The enemy were defeated though not subdued, and another detachment of two hundred rifles under my command was sent into the Ahmednuggur district. These Bheels, though badly armed, with matchlocks, spears, and swords, were formidable by sheer numbers. They were swift-footed, and lightly clad with only a loin-cloth, while our soldiers were strapped up in uniform, with stout boots, and carried heavy rifles and ammunition. Thus we were much handicapped, and often after making a forced march of some forty miles we found that the enemy had gone off some twenty-five miles in another direction, having been apprised of our approach by their spies. We therefore adopted a ruse, as it was difficult to bring them to bay. On one of these fruitless expeditions, finding they had bolted, we gave out that it was hopeless to catch them, and therefore returned home. This we knew would be reported at once to them by their spies, and, as we correctly anticipated, they would not leave their hiding-place, *Bheel-wara,* some twenty miles off. After marching for some miles towards our old camp, we halted, and rested for a few hours, lying *perdu* without light or fires, and then quietly moved off in the direction of their haunts, and arriving there in the early dawn, we caught them nicely by surprise, and inflicted severe loss on them, several being killed and wounded.

We subsequently proceeded by orders to Nassick, an ancient city in the neighbourhood of which is Trimbuk *the Holy*, where there are some handsome Hindoo temples of great sanctity; and as one of the Brahmin priests had been convicted of using grossly seditious language, inciting the people to rise, a severe example was deemed necessary, and he was sentenced to death. One of my companies, with a European officer, with loaded arms, was sent to act as a guard at the execution. It was a ticklish affair, for the people were very bigoted, and it was feared a rescue might be attempted. Thanks, however, to the steadiness, loyalty, and discipline of my men, who showed no sympathy with traitors, though among them were several of high caste in the ranks, the sentence was duly carried out, though the inhabitants showed their disgust by their sullen looks.

I may here mention that the arch-fiend Nana Sahib (the adopted heir of the Peishwah, or former ruler of the Deccan), and the perpetrator of the awful Cawnpore massacre, came originally with his family from this very neighbourhood.

About this time one of my subalterns, Lieutenant (now Colonel) Glasspoole, when on outpost duty at Dindorée, hearing that the insurgent Bheels—numbering about one thousand—were on their way to attack the small town of Peint, where there was a civil treasury and jail, feebly guarded by only a small body of police, at once on his own responsibility (there was no time for reference, the case being very urgent) made a forced march of over forty miles with some forty men, and arrived just in time to save the town from being looted, and the treasury from being plundered, and the prisoners released from jail! I made a strong report of this to the authorities, dwelling on the promptness and valuable services rendered by this officer with so small a party, but beyond receiving the thanks of the Governor in Council, he got nothing, whereas in my opinion he well deserved promotion or staff employ!

On the 17th December I returned to Wunee—a picturesque little place, which I made my headquarters. Here I spent the closing day of the eventful year 1857. On New Year's Eve, being in a serious and contemplative mood, I issued from my tent about midnight; it was a radiant night, the moon nearly at its full, and the blue canopy of heaven, bespangled with numerous brilliant stars, seemed engaged in a grand Hallelujah, "declaring the glory of God," as it ushered in the New Year! All was still in my little encampment almost hidden from view in a *tope*, or grove of mango trees, watered by a small and clear stream; dusky groups of sipahees, muleteers, and servants lay slumbering around the half-extinguished watch-fires; not a sound was heard, save the measured tread of my sentry near my tent. Facing me to the right extended the dark outline of the Khandeish Hills, a massive range of fantastic forms, while towering conspicuous above all was Shufter Sing, a gigantic mass of rock, in the immediate vicinity of which our active enemy found a comparatively safe retreat, and eluded us for a time.

On one occasion, accompanied by another officer, I made a military reconnaissance to this hill, taking with me a strong armed escort, in case we should meet some of this light-footed gentry; but we saw nothing of them, and the affair turned out a little picnic.

Being now all alone, as my officers were away on outpost duty, and having few books or papers and much leisure, and feeling solitary, I deemed it best to occupy my time by writing up my journal (which I had begun when entering upon my military career), from whence these notes are taken.

Early in March I received instructions to proceed with the rest of my detachment and a small party of irregular horse to the small town of Toka, on the banks of the Godavery River, to guard an important ford there, and prevent any body of rebels (Rohillas) and others from the Nizam's territory from crossing to our side and causing disturbances. As this was in close proximity to a turbulent district which was in sympathy with the rebels, I slept with a loaded revolver under my pillow, as well as my sword and uniform within reach.

Formerly there was a Bheel Corps, raised from these very people, on the principle of "Set a thief to catch a thief," and it answered very well, the country being comparatively quiet, till in an evil hour the Government, from short-sighted economy, abolished it, and hence the trouble that has arisen. These men were armed with muskets and fairly trained, and they had the good fortune to have for their Adjutant, Lieutenant Outram, then a young subaltern, who first brought himself into prominent notice by his good work among them and the great influence he acquired over them. He used to take them out on his hunting expeditions, and many stories are told of his prowess; as, for example, how on one occasion a tiger, who was the terror of the district, had been traced into a cave where none of the natives would go. Outram, however, went in on his hands and knees, rifle in hand, and the tiger was so startled at seeing this strange apparition that he jumped clean over him; and Outram, turning quickly round, shot him dead! Another time there was a huge bear which had taken refuge in some jungle bushes, and would not move in spite of stones, so Outram jumped down from a rock some ten feet high, close to Bruin, who stood up on his hind legs to give him a hug, and was shot. In fact, the natives looked upon Outram as a veritable *roostum* (hero) and a superior being.

There were several successful engagements in this district and Khandeish, including that of Ambapawnee, where we suffered some loss, one officer being killed and three wounded; but the enemy were quite disheartened and disbanded, many of their chiefs being killed, so that the campaign was practically at an end.

At this period I occasionally went out deerstalking, doing

110

my morning ride in the neighbouring country, where there was much game—black buck, antelopes, etc.—and on one occasion I severely wounded a buck, and galloped in chase after him, revolver in hand; but, though he had a broken leg, he managed to escape. These deer are very shy and wary, and the best way to get at them is to hire a native cart drawn by oxen, to which they are accustomed and take little notice of, and quietly slip out behind, and thus get a pretty fair shot at them.

The celebrated Caves of Ellora were not very far off, but, to my regret, I was unable to leave my post and visit them.

About the middle of June I received orders to proceed with my detachment to the Satpoora Hills and the head of the Scindwah Ghaut, where I took up my quarters at the travellers' bungalow. Thus ended the Bheel campaign.

Soon after my arrival, that fine regiment the 92nd Gordon Highlanders passed through in bullock wagons *en route* to Mhow, and I had the pleasure of entertaining the Colonel (Lockhart) and one of his captains (Bethune). The Colonel gave us an amusing account of an absurd scene on the way up with his men who were quite new to the country. It seems that one night, being encamped near a jungle, he heard a great stir, and observed that the carts had been hastily placed in a circle, forming a kind of stockade or laager. On inquiring the cause, a sergeant gravely remarked that, hearing the cry of jackals close by, they had adopted this precaution to guard against the attack of wild beasts, for, added the Scotch sergeant sagely, "Anybody acquaint wi' nat'ral history kens weel that the jackal is the lion's provider; and where he is, the lion is not far off." But there were no lions in that part, in point of fact!

Soon after, I joined my regiment at Mhow, just before the setting in of the monsoon, and was warmly greeted by my brother officers, and was glad to find that our old Colonel was now a Major-General and C.B. in command of the division.

I had some difficulty in finding a house, but was successful at last. After reporting myself through the Adjutant to my commanding officer, I resumed my former appointment as interpreter to my own regiment, and I was also appointed interpreter to the Gordon Highlanders through the kind offices of Colonel Lockhart, and served with them during the great Mutiny of which the next chapter will give an account.

CHAPTER 14

The Indian Mutiny

STAMPING IT OUT

In the last chapter I mentioned the almost insuperable difficulty of finding a vacant bungalow or house at Mhow, owing to the exceptional number of troops of all arms then assembled there. However, our obliging surgeon, Doctor Ritchie, invited me to pitch my tent in his compound, and be his guest till I could find some other place; and at length a good friend offered me his outhouse or vacant office, and I was only too thankful to get the shelter of a roof, now that the monsoon had set in.

À *propos* of our worthy doctor above referred to, who was a fine specimen of a stalwart Scot, being over six feet, and who was much esteemed in our regiment, I may mention an incident which occurred when he was with the rear-guard in one of the Afghan campaigns. This guard was attacked, and on the officer in charge being wounded, he took command, and charged the enemy with such energy and boldness that they were quickly routed. He received the special thanks of the General, and earned afterwards the sobriquet of the fighting doctor.

Mhow is a favourite station, having a temperate climate, and it was the headquarters of a division commanded by our old Colonel (Major-General Honner, C.B.), who made a special request to Government to have his own regiment (4th Rifles) under his command, which was granted.

This station, from its exceptional position, being within striking distance of the most disturbed districts in Central India, was a good base to start from; for, though the neck of the Mutiny was broken, there were still large bodies of trained soldiers of the rebels with guns and cavalry about the country, keeping up a constant agitation and causing the greatest mischief by buoying up the hopes of the disaffected.

It was therefore imperative to stamp out these smouldering fires of rebellion and administer stern retribution before the country could be considered as pacified and British supremacy reasserted in the face of the world.

As soon, therefore, as the monsoon or heavy rains were practically over, several flying columns (as they were called) were organised—composed of artillery, cavalry, and infantry, and spread over the country to co-operate with each other by harassing, hemming in, and cutting up these rebel forces. To one of these columns I was attached as Interpreter and Staff Officer. It was composed of the headquarters wing of the 92nd Gordon Highlanders, a battery of European artillery under Captain Le Marchand, a squadron of the 3rd Bombay Light Cavalry, and the 19th Regiment Native Infantry under Major Barrow, the whole being commanded by Colonel Lockhart, 92nd, acting as Brigadier, altogether about twelve hundred men of all arms, and with that distinguished and enterprising young officer, Lieutenant Evelyn Wood (now Field-Marshal, V.C., G.C.B.), acting as Intelligence Officer in command of a troop of the Bombay Light Cavalry.

We left Mhow about the end of August, being accompanied by Major Hutchinson, the Assistant Political Agent, subsequently by Captain Gordon Cumming, and passing through Indore, the capital of H.H. the Maharajah Holkar, one of the principal Mahratta chiefs (whose loyalty was somewhat doubtful), we duly reached Oojein, on the river Seprie, a very ancient city, with many fine Hindoo temples and a remarkable gateway of great antiquity. The inhabitants were struck dumb with surprise on seeing for the first time in their lives our fine kilted Highlanders!

Passing through Mehidpore, where formerly Sir John Malcolm obtained a brilliant victory, we reached Augur, once a beautiful station, but which had been destroyed by the mutinous Bengal Sipahees, who killed some of their officers and set fire to the place. There is a fine lake here, having a pretty little island, where one of our elephants, which had suddenly become mad (*must*, as it is termed), swam off to, having killed two natives and put to flight some of the Highlanders, who with fixed bayonets attempted to stop him, and he had eventually to be killed by a round shot from one of our guns, as bullets seemed to have little effect upon him!

We heard that the rebels were in *great force*, about eighteen thousand, some forty miles off, and had forced a Rajah to join them with his guns, and they were commanded by the Nawab of Banda.

The Brigadier directed the troop of native cavalry under Lieutenant E. Wood to reconnoitre the enemy, and he learnt that their advance guard had only a day or two before quitted this neighbourhood after plundering a village. As the enemy numbered several thousands of trained soldiers, with many guns and a large body of cavalry, our position was somewhat critical; but our excellent Brigadier was quite equal to the occasion, and with sound judgement decided neither to advance nor retire, but to stand fast where we were, and we at once entrenched ourselves. We made a trench round our camp, and throwing up the earth dug out as a parapet, planted our guns at the angles, and quietly awaited the attack, in the meanwhile sending for some immediate reinforcements to Mhow.

The enemy, emboldened by our taking up a defensive position, advanced within a few miles, as though making a feint to attack us; but, seeing we were not dismayed, they moved off, deeming "discretion the better part of valour." Had we made the slightest retrograde movement, they would have come down upon us like wolves, and by sheer weight of numbers might have overwhelmed us; but our bold front saved us.

On the 10th September we were reinforced, to our great satisfaction, by more troops from Mhow, including my own regiment, and the two columns joined together formed the Malwa Field Force, under the command of Major-General Michel, C.B., to whom I also acted as Interpreter, Staff Officer, and extra A.D.C.

No time was lost in now taking the offensive and pursuing the enemy. After many forced marches, we succeeded in bringing them to bay at a beautiful spot called Rajghur. We found them drawn up in battle array on the brow of a hill, numbering about ten thousand men, including a large body of cavalry and some forty guns, altogether looking very formidable and imposing. They at once opened a vigorous cannonade upon us as we deployed into line, covered by our skirmishers, and steadily advanced to attack their position, the round shot falling thick around us.

Meanwhile, our artillery, under Captain Le Marchand, by the precision of its fire, was doing great execution, the enemy being evidently staggered by it. At length, seeing our infantry advancing as steadily as if on parade, in spite of all obstructions, and that our rifles were brought to bear upon them, they lost heart, broke, and fled, being closely pursued by our cavalry, who killed some two hundred of them.

Such was the action of Rajghur, fought on the 15th September 1858. It lasted about five hours, and we captured twenty-eight guns, some of heavy calibre, and inflicted severe loss on the enemy, while our own casualties were comparatively small. The heat, however, was truly awful; several of our men, both European and native, had sunstroke, one officer of the cavalry being killed, and an officer of the rifles had to be invalided, and eventually died.

The rifles had the honour of escorting the captured guns to Mhow, and doubtless the mere transit through the disturbed districts (being a palpable proof of our victory) was not without its moral effect on the disaffected.

Having buried our dead, we continued our march and pursuit towards Sehore, the capital of the small independent State of Bhopaul, which was then threatened, the Begum or Sovereign Queen being a loyal ally of ours. From Bhopaul turning northwards we crossed the river Parbutee, passed through Nursinghur, and reached Bersia, where we halted for a day, to the great relief of all. We learned that the rebels had gone to Seronge, where there are great jungles, and thence to Bundelcund, a mountainous country, where pursuit would be difficult.

Besides our field force there were several other columns in the field co-operating with us to drive the enemy towards us; but, with their remarkable powers of marching great distances, they often eluded us.

On the 29th September I saw for the first time in my life a most brilliant comet with a beautiful tail. It is a curious circumstance that the natives have the same opinion of its appearance as our old astronomers had in past time, that it denotes war and disaster; and one of our native officers pointed out to me the fact that its head was always pointed in the direction of the rebels, thus denoting disaster to them. We therefore accepted the omen as good to ourselves, and gravely drew the attention of the inhabitants to it. The comet remained visible for many days. All turned out just as we wished for on the morning of the 9th October, on reaching Mungrowlie, we learnt from our cavalry vedettes that the enemy's advance guard was in sight and moving towards us. Our General sounded the "Assembly," and we very soon came face to face with them.

On our horse artillery galloping to the front and delivering a few rounds of shot and shell, they fell back on their main body, which was posted on an eminence near the village of Mungrowlie. Here massed in dense columns, their front covered by skirmishers and supported by artillery, they awaited our approach, while their powerful body of cavalry protected their flanks, quite prepared to pounce upon us should we be worsted. No time was lost on our part, for we deployed into line as we advanced rapidly to the attack, which was vigorously pushed forward, our skirmishers and artillery doing great execution, and creating much confusion and disorder among the enemy. In the meanwhile, however, while we were thus busily engaged in front, a large body of the enemy's cavalry (in which lay their strength and our weakness) had managed, by making a great detour and under cover of the smoke, to get unperceived on our flank and rear. Brigadier Lockhart, to whom I acted as A.D.C., sent me to inform the General of this fact. I galloped off, and on my way back I saw, to my surprise, that the enemy's cavalry were close upon us. I at once reported this to the General, and pointed out where they were. Without a moment's delay he set the splendid squadron of the 17th Lancers, under Sir W. Gordon, at them.

It was a fine sight to witness these "Death or Glory Boys," as they are called (from their wearing a death's head and cross-bones on their appointments), gallantly charge a body of cavalry several times their number and put them to flight. Moreover, I was pleased that the enemy got a lesson, for on my way to the General I noticed a *doolie*, or litter, with an unfortunate bearer killed, and on lifting up the flap, saw a poor sick Highlander breathe his last, having been speared by these cowardly wretches.

The enemy were commanded by the celebrated Tantia Topee, their most active and capable General, and the conception of this cavalry attack on our flank and rear was doubtless his, and if it had been pushed with more dash and daring, and as a surprise, it would probably have succeeded. In this second action with us the enemy were completely defeated, with the loss of some six hundred men and several guns, and so panic-stricken were they that they fled across the river Betwa up to their necks in water!

Crossing the river, we advanced on Balapait, a large town, which we found deserted. Next day we marched on Malthun (thirty-six miles from the large station of Saugor in the Bengal Presidency), and were here joined by reinforcements of cavalry.

Late at night news was brought us by our spies that the enemy were at Sindwaho, about fourteen miles off, having been reinforced by troops under the Rao Saheb, a nephew of the infamous Nana, and it was added that they had sworn together the most sacred of oaths to fight to the last, and annihilate us! Our energetic commander determined at once to give them the opportunity they desired before their courage should evaporate. Accordingly, we marched at 4 a.m. without delay.

On the 19th October I had been sent on by the General ahead of the advance guard to assist the Assistant Quarter-Master General as interpreter, and we two had a narrow escape of being made prisoners on this occasion; for as we advanced, finding no signs of an enemy, we were making straight for a large grove or *tope* of trees about a mile off, near which in a large ravine the whole rebel army were lying concealed! Fortunately for us, one of the two native horsemen with us elicited this important fact from an old woman working in a field, and I caught sight of the glimmer of some spears there, corroborating this; so we fell back on our advance guard, and reported the circumstance to the General.

As our little army advanced, the rebels leisurely emerged from their concealment and took up a strong position on some rising ground near the village of Sindwaho, their right resting on and being protected by a grove of trees. Taking, as usual, the initiative, we advanced to the attack, and on

119

our arriving within range a masked battery from the *tope* of trees opened a heavy fire upon us with shot and shell. Our troop of horse artillery, followed by Le Marchand's horse battery, galloped to the front, each guarded by a troop of cavalry, and were quickly engaged, while the main body of the cavalry under De Salis were posted on the right flank, Mayne's Horse being on the left, and the infantry formed in line to the left rear. Soon the action became general, the enemy's round shot and shell falling unpleasantly near us, while our artillery replied with interest and much greater effect. Ere long symptoms of confusion and disorder were visible among the enemy's ranks, upon which a general advance was ordered, the Enfields doing good service, while the cavalry pressed on their flanks, charging bodies of them and thus completing their rout. We pursued them with our horse artillery and cavalry for some miles to the banks of the Jumna, the whole distance being strewn with their slain. As I was acting as extra A.D.C. to the General, I accompanied him to the end of the pursuit. While galloping along I caught sight of a handsome *palanquin* (litter), and riding up to it pistol in hand, looked in, and found the bird had flown (H.H. the Nawab of Banda himself, as we learnt afterwards), and the only thing I could find inside was a beautiful riding-whip made of coloured seed-pearls, which I secured and presented to the General for his daughter, as he admired it very much.

In this action, which was the sharpest we had with the rebels and in which they made the most determined stand, they mustered upwards of two thousand cavalry, some thousands of infantry, and several guns. Their loss was very great, amounting to six hundred or seven hundred men, with all their guns, and quantities of ammunition, horses, camels, etc.; while our own loss was small, including an officer of the 8th Hussars, who was killed. Thus ended the battle of Sindwaho, in which campaign the gallant Malwa Field Force gained great kudos eventually, our General (Michel) being knight-ed, our Brigadier (Lockhart) and other Brigadiers receiving the Companionship of the Bath, and the officers of the Staff, including myself, were mentioned in the despatches, and a medal granted to all the troops engaged in suppressing the great Mutiny.

CHAPTER 15

The Close of the Indian Mutiny

After their signal defeat at Sindwaho the Rebel Army fled northward, and we learnt that great dissensions had arisen among them, the men openly accusing their chiefs of cowardice, while the infantry bitterly upbraided the cavalry for deserting them in their hour of need. The result was that a large portion of the infantry separated from the main body and dispersed in disgust.

On the 20th October, the day after the battle, we marched to Beora, and thence to Lullutpore, formerly a station for the Gwalior Contingent, whose European officers had been made close prisoners, and the cantonment plundered and burnt by these very men we were hunting down.

On our arrival there, we learnt that, finding themselves hemmed in by our various columns, they had doubled south towards Bhopaul, with wonderful rapidity. As it was of great importance that we should frustrate their designs, our energetic General pursued them with great vigour, making three most trying forced marches, and he again succeeded in catching them at the village of Kuraee. They were taken quite by surprise, as they were marching right across our front. We attacked them at once, and they made comparatively little stand, being disheartened and demoralised by their numerous reverses. We divided their force into two parts, one of which, with their treasure chest guarded by their best cavalry, managed to escape. The other portion was severely handled by our artillery and cavalry. Among the slain was one of their most noted chiefs, while others were taken prisoners, and shot by sentence of court-martial.

This, our last action with the rebels, took place on the 25th October 1858, and as we learnt that the rebels were now completely broken up and mere fugitives, the General decided on pursuing them with his cavalry only, leaving the infantry brigade behind under Brigadier Lockhart, with whom I was directed to remain.

I took advantage of this brief respite to visit the celebrated Topes of Bhilsa, in the neighbourhood, of which Captain Cunningham of the Bengal Engineers has given a most interesting account. They are huge mounds of masonry, Buddhist monuments of remote antiquity, dating, it is said, centuries before Christ, and well worth a visit.

One of the greatest difficulties I had to encounter as interpreter and staff officer was the postal department, which was placed under my charge, with only two native clerks to assist me. One of these I required to help me in sorting the letters, European and native, of the various columns; my other clerk, who fortunately owned a pony, I employed in organising *tappauls*, or letter carriers, with the headman of each village, to be forwarded to the various columns, under penalty of severe punishment and fines if neglected; and I am glad to say this was carried out to the General's satisfaction, which relieved my mind.

I was congratulating myself on getting a little rest after all my recent fatigue, when I received a peremptory order from the Assistant Adjutant-General to join General Michel without delay. This was no easy matter, as he was proceeding by forced marches and had four days' start. Fortunately, however, a squadron of the Guzerat Horse, under my friend Captain Buckle, passed through *en route* to join the General, and I obtained permission to go with them, and after making a tremendous march of sixty-four miles, we arrived on the banks of the Nerbuddah, only to find that the General had left that very morning! However, I at last joined him on the 25th October.

On reporting myself, I at once resumed my duties.

About this period our gracious Queen issued a proclamation offering amnesty to all rebels who should surrender by a given date, excluding those only who had been guilty of the murder of Europeans, and several accepted these terms, including the Nawab of Banda, against whom we had been fighting, and who, finding himself surrounded by us, surrendered.

The rebels being now completely disposed of and all their guns captured, and no enemy worthy of the name to contend with, the General decided to return to Mhow, recrossing the Nerbuddah, and arriving there on the 30th November, covered with glory and dust. Right glad were we all to have a roof over our heads!

To sum up. During this short but brilliant campaign we had undergone arduous and continuous marches, amounting to something like one thousand miles at the most trying season of the year, and under a deadly sun. We had defeated the flower of the rebel army, some fifteen thousand men, under their best leaders, in four successive engagements, and captured all their guns! Nothing could exceed the spirit, zeal, and soldierly bearing of all ranks under the very severe hardships they had to undergo, as well as their cheerfulness and admirable conduct throughout, which elicited the warmest thanks not only of His Excellency the Commander-in-Chief and the Governor-General, but also of both Houses of Parliament.

As to that miscreant Nana Sahib—though he was never captured, yet there were good reasons for believing that he was hunted down for the large price set on his head, and eventually perished miserably of fever in the Nepaul jungles. As to Tantia Topee, the great rebel leader who gave us so much trouble, he was taken prisoner, having been betrayed by one of his own countrymen, and after conviction by sentence of a military commission, he was executed.

All those actually employed in the suppression of this great Mutiny received a bounty of six months' *batta*, extra pay, and eventually a medal and clasp was awarded.

Soon after my arrival at Mhow, I was directed to proceed to Indore in command of a wing of my regiment, while I was still permitted to hold my appointment as interpreter to H.M.'s 92nd Highlanders.

On the day after my arrival at Indore I called officially on the Resident or Agent of the Governor-General, Sir Robert Hamilton, Bart., who received me very courteously, and placed some elephants at the disposal of myself and brother-officers, to visit the city and the palace of H.H. the Maharajah Holkar. The gardens called the *Lai Bagh* are laid out in the Italian style, with elegant summer-houses, fountains, etc.

On Christmas Day 1858 we had a little social gathering at our mess, sitting after dinner round a wood fire, endeavouring to feel as home-like as we could under the circumstances, and with the comfortable assurance that we had fairly earned the *otium* after our severe campaigning, though it was but the ghost of an English Christmastide!

Early in 1859 I was relieved of the command of the left wing at Indore, and, returning to Mhow, resumed my appointment as interpreter to the Gordon Highlanders.

Soon after, orders were received for the 92nd Highlanders to proceed to Jhansi and relieve the 3rd Bombay European Regiment there—somewhat unwelcome news, as the heat of that station is proverbial. We left Mhow on the 2nd March with much regret, and, as the distance to Jhansi was something like three hundred miles, we had about a month's march before us. Passing through Tonk, we reached Sarungpore on the 8th, and on the 10th we passed H.M. 64th Regiment *en route* to Bombay, and we gave them three hearty cheers, as they had done gallant service under Havelock at the relief of Lucknow, as well as in Persia. At length, after passing through Goonah, we arrived at Jhansi on the 7th April, and relieved the 3rd Europeans, with whom we dined on the day of arrival.

This young regiment did excellent service during the height of the Mutiny, with the Central India Field Force, under Sir Hugh Rose, especially at the siege and capture of Jhansi, and was subsequently commanded by me as H.M. 109th Regiment. This place with its fort possesses a most unenviable notoriety, for here upwards of sixty of our brave countrymen and women defended themselves most bravely against overwhelming numbers, and when compelled to surrender *conditionally,* by dire necessity, were foully butchered at the instigation of that she-devil, the Rhanee of Jhansi. But a stern and righteous retribution awaited them, for, on the capture of this place by Sir H. Rose's force, the principal agents and instigators of this foul and bloody deed were hung on the gallows erected on the very spot where our poor fellow-countrymen and women suffered so terribly.

During the march the heat was intense, ranging up to 96° in my tent, and as I had a touch of sunstroke at the latter stage, I travelled in a *doolie,* being on the sick list. Not appearing to gain strength, I applied for and obtained two months' leave to proceed to Mussoorie and the hills north of Dehra.

Accordingly, taking leave of Colonel Lockhart and the officers of H.M. 92nd Gordon Highlanders, for whom I shall always feel a warm regard, I proceeded with a friend to Gwalior, which is remarkable for its impregnable fortress, built on a huge solid rock, and belonging to H.H. the Maharajah Scindia.

Thence we proceeded to Agra, where I put up with my old schoolfellow and connection, Captain W. Mylne, from whom and his wife I received a cordial welcome.

I, of course, visited the celebrated Taj Mahal, a mausoleum erected by the Emperor Akbar to his favourite wife; but I will not attempt to describe it, as this has been often done, yet I cannot refrain from saying that its actual size is dwarfed by its exquisite proportions, dazzling purity, and elegance of the *tout ensemble,* and it suggests to the eye that the whole could be put under a glass case like the Crystal Palace

The large fortress of Agra was the home of many refugees who sought its safe and strong shelter during the height of the Mutiny, and successfully repulsed all attacks.

Leaving Agra on the 19th by *dak gharee* with my friend, and crossing the river Jumna by the fine bridge of boats, we arrived at Meerut on the afternoon of the following day.

This fine station has the unenviable notoriety of being the place where the Mutiny broke out in full force on the 10th May 1857 *(Dies Iræ)*. From here it spread rapidly through-out India, assuming colossal proportions. I drove about the cantonment, visiting the Lines occupied by these mutineers who set fire to the station and committed various atrocities. The Lines were now more worthily occupied by the faith-ful little Goorkhas (hill-men), who did such excellent service throughout the Mutiny.

Being here obliged to part with my fellow-traveller, I pro-ceeded alone by dak to Rajpore, at the foot of the Hills, and about daybreak on the morning of the 25th April arrived at Mussoorie in time for breakfast at Smiles's Hotel.

As I rode up the ghaut I was much struck by the beautiful scenery around, and also with the picturesque appearance of Mussoorie and Landour. In place, however, of being a plateau like Mahabuleshwar Hills, I found to my surprise that except the Mall, there was scarcely a level piece of ground! Many of the houses resembled Swiss chalets of a superior kind, and are mostly built on the sloping sides of the hills, or perched like eagles' nests on some crag.

I was not long in obtaining my first view of the snowy range of the mighty Himalayas "glistening in their virgin snow," and it was indeed a grand and glorious sight. The finest view is I think obtained from the Hospital, the highest ground at Landour.

I passed the time very pleasantly at Mussoorie, being made Honorary Member of the excellent Himalaya Club, one of the best managed in India. I also visited that excellent institution, the Lawrence Asylum, for the benefit of the sons and daughters of our European soldiers—a blessed boon, due entirely to the generosity and initiative of Sir Henry Lawrence, his family and friends. I had the honour of seeing this noble Christian soldier at Mooltan, when on his way to Lahore.

The entire suppression of the Indian Mutiny being now a *fait accompli,* leave to visit Europe, which had been withheld, was thrown open, and as I was entitled to mine, having served ten years in India, and my health being far from strong, I applied for the same.

Thunderstorms are prevalent here at this season, and we experienced a terrible one—a grand sight, which I viewed from the terrace in front of the Club, the lightning on that occasion striking a Hindoo temple, and doing much damage. One evening I rode out to Waverley Hill, and obtained a most lovely view of the Snowy Range by sunset, the snow-capped peaks being bathed in a rich crimson hue, while the hills around covered with the graceful Himalaya pines (Deodara) stood out in bold relief.

Early in June 1860 I obtained three years' furlough to Europe, and was also granted a month's leave preparatory thereto. I wrote to my agents at Calcutta to secure my passage to Suez by the P. & O. steamer of the 18th July.

I left Mussoorie on the 24th June, in company with a friend, and rode down to the foot of the Hills (having to my regret had to part with my little Arab, which had done me good service), and thence drove to Dehra, visiting the fine tea-plantations there.

Resuming our journey by *palki*, and travelling all night, I awoke about daybreak to find myself alone in the jungles, the bearers having decamped, and the rain descending in torrents. However, I soon found them under shelter with a fire, and quietly smoking their pipes, and quickly stirring them up, reached Delhi on the morning of the 27th June.

What deep and conflicting emotions does that very name recall—as the hotbed, focus, and grand rendezvous of the rebellion, where in the fatal month of May the most fearful atrocities were perpetrated, the native troops murdering their officers and the whole Christian population, sparing neither age nor sex. Let us not dwell on this hideous picture, but rather call to mind with pride the heroic deeds of the Avenging Army, who, within four months after, besieged and captured the accursed city, though alas! at a terrible sacrifice of life, the noble-hearted General Nicholson, the Hero of Delhi, being among the number.

I went over the ground where our army were posted along the Ridge, and examined with interest the principal points. I visited the palace where the old puppet king resided with his infamous sons and grandsons, and also rode out to the Emperor Humayon's tomb, where the gallant Hodson captured the latter.

Quitting Delhi with my friend on the 28th, we, during the night, met with a serious accident, through the carelessness of our dak driver and the viciousness of a shying horse, by which the carriage fell over an embankment into the canal! Fortunately, we were both awake at the time, and seeing what was about to happen, we took a flying leap out of each door, and escaped with only a few bruises and somewhat stunned, while the wretched driver was pitched into the canal, the carriage being smashed; we had to walk some distance to the next stage, and procure a fresh carriage.

We reached Agra on the 29th, where I was again hospitably entertained by my friends Captain and Mrs. Mylne, the former being commissariat officer there.

The heat was intense, and we had punkahs going night and

129

day, a thing almost unheard of in our Western Presidency; but my friend had a fine swimming bath in his compound, which was a great treat, especially at such a season. Before leaving Agra I took another look by moonlight at the wonderful Taj, which looked more ethereal and fairy-like than ever!

Taking farewell of my kind friends, I resumed my journey by *dak*, and on the 8th July arrived at Cawnpore!

Cawnpore! What a thrill of horror does, that name conjure up! The entrenchment where General Wheeler and his devoted band so splendidly defended themselves—a mere ditch—was pointed out to me by an artilleryman, and also the awful slaughterhouse where upwards of two hundred women and children were so foully butchered by that fiend in human form Nana Sahib. I cannot trust myself to describe the feelings excited in my mind while gazing on this dreadful scene where the fearful tragedy was enacted. A beautiful memorial cross has been erected over the spot and the well where the poor victims were thrown, which is overshadowed by a lovely pure white marble angel figure with outstretched wings bending over, as it were in deep grief and sympathy, and is the work, I believe, of Baron Marochetti, and bearing a most touching inscription; this sacred spot is enclosed by railings and carefully kept. Here for the first time I saw the sacred river Ganges (*Gunga*), so much venerated and worshipped by millions of Hindoos, which has its sources in the Himalaya Mountains.

Quitting this city of sad memories, I proceeded by rail to Allahabad, situated at the junction of the rivers Jumna and Ganges, where there is a very strong fortress, which was saved from falling into the hands of the rebels by the energy and promptitude of the late General Neill of the Madras Army. Resuming my journey by *dak*, I reached Benares, the Holy in the eyes of all Hindoos, on the morning of the 10th July: it is beautifully situated on the Ganges, and adorned by innumerable temples. Leaving Benares and travelling all night (the heat being too intense during the day), I reached Raneegunge, whence by train to Calcutta, on the afternoon of the 13th, and crossing the Hooghly, proceeded in a carriage to Alipore, on the outskirts, when I was kindly welcomed by my friends and connections, Major and Mrs. C. Herbert. The former held a political appointment, being in charge of the ex-King and Princes of Oude, and received the thanks of both Houses of Parliament for his heroic defence of Attock.

CHAPTER 16

Furlough and Promotion

Calcutta, the capital of British India and the seat of the Supreme Government, has been styled the City of Palaces, and certainly, from its immense wealth, great size, and population, its splendid public buildings and spacious *maidan*, or esplanade, it is very imposing. It is, however, by no means so picturesquely situated as Bombay, and its climate is unhealthy and enervating. In fact, Bombay from its greater salubrity, splendid bay and seaboard, fine harbour, proximity to Europe, and its claim as the great commercial emporium, as well as advantages of situation, may almost be regarded as the real capital of our Indian empire. Indeed, this question has been mooted of late years both in India and at home.

I was much struck by the palatial appearance of Government House, where the Viceroy resides, and also by the Suddur Adawlut College, the Ochterlony Column, and Fort William; the last named is a very extensive *bonâ fide* fortress of the first class with excellent barracks, and having accommodation for some four thousand men. The Cathedral also is a fine building. The fashionable evening drive is the Course, where the wealth and beauty of Calcutta most do congregate.

Having at length made all my arrangements, dismissed my faithful valet (who had been with me for many years) with a well-earned *douceur*, and bade adieu to my kind friends, I found myself on the 18th July 1860 on board the P. & O. steamer *Nubia* steaming down the Hooghly, and for the second time turned my back, by no means reluctantly, on the shores of India.

I found among my fellow-passengers Colonel Michel, who was the brother of my old chief, General Sir John Michel, K.C.B., on whose staff I served during the Indian Mutiny, and we soon fraternised, as we were also sharing the same cabin on the main deck.

On the evening of the 23rd we arrived off Madras. The view of this city from the sea is somewhat tame. The long, low shore is covered with date trees, and the sea rolls with a heavy surf. There are some fine-looking buildings, including the Custom House, railway terminus, lighthouse, Fort St. George, and many handsome houses. I was interested in the catamarans, of which I had heard much. They are mere rafts made of rough logs of timber knit together, and propelled by a couple of nearly naked men, who appear to be sitting or standing on the water. In these rude and frail barques they venture fearlessly through the most tremendous surf.

Leaving Madras on the following day, and emerging from the Bay of Bengal, we coasted the lovely island of Ceylon, and cast anchor off Point de Galle; touched at Aden on the 7th August, and soon after entering the Red Sea we sighted the wreck of the P. & O. Steamer *Alma,* lost here some months before. Some of the unfortunate officers of that ill-fated vessel came on board, and appeared very wretched as they told us that they had nothing to eat for some days but coconuts and sugar! We gave them some provisions, as they could not leave their unenviable position.

The heat in the Red Sea at this time of the year is intense, and as it was impossible to sleep below in the cabins, all the passengers, male and female, slept on deck, a large ship's sail-awning being placed between them. We arrived at Suez on the 14th, and the same afternoon proceeded by rail to Cairo, and on to Alexandria, securing my passage by the French steamer for Leghorn, where I arrived on the 1st September.

As I was suffering from rheumatism and nervous debility, brought on by the trying campaign I had undergone, I was advised by my medical attendant to go to the mineral baths of Acqui (Casciana), where as children we used to go, and of which I had pleasant reminiscences. Accordingly, I proceeded there, with an old man-servant of the family to look after me. The country around there is most beautiful, and we drove through some ten miles of lovely scenery, the luscious grapes hanging in festoons all along the road—for it was the vintage season (*La vendemmia*), reminding me of Byron's lines—

Sweet is the vintage, when the show'ring grapes,
In Bacchanal profusion, reel to earth, purple and gushing!

What with the change of scene, the rest, and balmy air of *La bella Italia,* the beautiful land of my birth, for which and its warm-hearted people I have ever had a deep affection, together with the effects of the mineral baths, I derived some benefit, though my stay was short. I returned to Livorno, and early in October left for Marseilles, which I reached the second day, and from thence I went to Paris. My stay there was brief, and I arrived in London about the middle of October, right glad to find myself once more in dear old England. After reporting my arrival at the India House, and staying a week in town, I started for Scotland, to the banks of the bonnie Clyde, where my family then resided.

In the spring of the following year I contracted a severe rheumatic fever, and on consulting my kind friend, the late eminent and distinguished physician Sir James Simpson, I was recommended to go to Benrhydding Hydropathic Establishment, where on a previous visit I had derived much benefit. After a visit of six weeks, by persevering with the treatment I entirely got rid of my rheumatism. *Grazia Dio.*

My furlough was much spent in travelling about the country,

visiting various relatives and friends, and among other places in which I was much interested was the royal and ancient city of St. Andrews, where I lived, subsequently, with my parents.

It is a most picturesque old city, with the ruins of its fine Cathedral, St. Regulus Tower, and historic Castle. Here Mary Queen of Scots once resided. Being the seat of a well-known University, there were many eminent men of letters and talent there during my residence, including the late Sir David Brewster, to whom I had the honour of being introduced, as also Principals Tulloch and Shairp, Professor Flint, Dr. Boyd, the well-known author (A. K. H. B.); the brothers Drs. Robert and William Chambers, founders of *Chambers's Journal;* and Bishop Wordsworth of St. Andrews, who was tutor to the Right Honourable W. E. Gladstone.

But with many the great attraction of St. Andrews is that it is the headquarters of the great national game of golf. Its breezy links are nearly always crowded with players, and great matches for the championship are held here. I was duly initiated into the mysteries of this fascinating game by Tom Morris, the great champion player.

In the spring of 1862 I was staying at Edinburgh with relatives, and while there I had the pleasure of renewing my acquaintanceship with the little fair-haired girl I met in *Mid-desert* some eighteen years before (referred to in Chapter 1.), Miss Constance Wright, eldest daughter of James Wright, Esq., of Ainslie Place, Edinburgh. We were eventually married at St. John's Church there by her cousin, the Rev. R. Duckworth, now Canon of Westminster (D.D., C.V.O.), on 10th June 1862.

We went on our wedding tour to the Trossachs, Lochs Katrine and Lomond, and paid our first visit to my wife's venerable grandfather on the banks of the Clyde. From thence we proceeded to visit my sister and brother-in-law in their fine old seat of Guthrie in Forfarshire, and afterwards to my bride's father's residence, Fern Tower, in the beautiful Strathearn district of Perthshire.

Here during the autumn I had some good shooting and occasional rides, visiting Drummond Castle and other places of note in the neighbourhood.

But our visit, being of a farewell nature prior to our return to India, was somewhat saddened by the thought of leaving those near and dear to us. We were, however, cheered by a piece of great good news, for by the reconquest of India after the Mutiny the destinies of that great Empire were transferred from the Honourable East India Company (who were kind and liberal masters) to the Crown. The Indian Army being included, there was a consequent amalgamation of the European portion with the Royal Army. As the officers had the option of either joining the Indian Staff Corps, remaining local, or for general service, I applied for the last, which proved a fortunate hit, for I believe I obtained greater promotion than almost any other officer, being transferred from fourth Captain in an Indian regiment to be senior Major of H.M. 109th Regiment. I was warmly congratulated by my friends, and it was also an agreeable surprise to me.

About the middle of October we paid our last farewell visit to my dear parents at St. Andrews, when I saw my venerable father, alas! for the last time. We proceeded to London to obtain my new uniform and to make our final arrangements, paying a short visit to some relatives who lived in a charming-villa called The Chalet, a model of a fine Swiss chalet, which belonged to Albert Smith, the great Alpine climber and popular lecturer.

About the end of October we bade adieu to old England and numerous friends, and crossing the Channel we reached Paris, where we stayed a few days as guests of a near relative of my wife's. This gave the latter an opportunity of seeing something of this gay city. Thence we proceeded to Marseilles.

As we were desirous not to proceed direct to Alexandria, but *viâ* Italy, we found that, according to the excellent arrangements of the steamers of the French *Messageries Imperi-*

ales, we could do so by taking circular tickets, giving us the option of stopping if we pleased at Florence, Rome, and Naples, and resuming our journey by subsequent steamers of the same company.

This boon we fully took advantage of, and it was a source of much pleasure to me to act as a *cicerone* to my wife on this her first visit to Italy. After a pleasant *séjour* at Florence and visiting old haunts of mine, we proceeded to Pisa, to enable her to see that splendid group of the Leaning Tower, Duomo, and Baptistery. I also paid a visit of homage to that noble patriot Garibaldi, who was there recovering from his wound at the ill-fated battle of Aspromonte. I found the grand old hero, for whom I have ever felt great admiration, lying on a couch surrounded by his family, and was kindly received by him. We conversed both in English and Italian, and at parting he shook me warmly by the hand, wishing me *buon viaggio,* and I was presented with his photo bearing his autograph, which I much prize. From Pisa we went to Rome, and thus I again found myself in the Eternal City after the lapse of several years.

When in St. Peter's we saw there the Crown Prince and Princess of Prussia (Princess Royal of England), and were fortunate in seeing the interesting Catacombs of St. Calixtus illuminated (a rare occurrence), having been lighted up for their special benefit by the Roman Government. We saw, of course, the noble Coliseum, the Forum, and other sights, and I heard also some splendid singing in one of the churches on the festival of St. Cecilia, the Patron Saint of Musicians. Retracing our steps by train to Civita Vecchia, we caught the steamer, and arrived at Naples the following morning, my wife being charmed with its magnificent bay.

After staying a week at Naples we again embarked for Messina, whence we proceeded by the French steamer to Alexandria. Our voyage, however, proved a somewhat disastrous one, for we encountered a heavy storm which, by injuring some of the machinery, disabled the vessel. We were in some danger, and forced to take refuge for repairs at Cyra, a small seaport in Greece.

However, in the circumstances we were not sorry to find ourselves on *terra firma* again, obtaining at the same time a glimpse of this classic land and its inhabitants.

There was at this time much enthusiasm in Greece at the proposal to make our young Prince Alfred their king, and when the inhabitants heard that there was an English field officer on board, I was waited upon by a deputation in their picturesque gala dress, who presented me with an address, and expressed in French the anxious, universal desire of their nation to that effect. I replied in the same language, thanking them for the compliment, offering my best wishes that their hopes and aspirations might be realised, in accordance with the welfare of their classic land.

I heard of a more amusing scene having occurred regarding this regal prospect in the man-of-war in which Prince Alfred served as a middy; for his companions, with their fondness for fun and practical jokes, constructed a tin crown in which they inserted lighted tallow candles, and placing it on his head, hailed him with mock solemnity as King of Greece!

The storm having abated, and the machinery repaired, we resumed our voyage, and duly reached Alexandria.

Owing, however, to the gross carelessness of the French officials, we found our baggage had been left behind; so, much to our inconvenience and annoyance, we were detained a fortnight longer at Alexandria till it eventually turned up. On opening her boxes, my wife, to our horror and dismay, discovered that her valuable jewel-case was empty; but fortunately the contents were found at the bottom of the trunk, the case having been burst open by the terrible jolting which the boxes had undergone! So we consoled ourselves by the saying, "All's well that ends well." We resumed our journey, and reached Bombay early in January 1863.

Here we were the guests of kind friends in their charming house of Love Grove.

This city has peculiar attractions and interest to my dear wife, being her natal place, endeared to her by tender associations of her childhood, as her parents resided here for some years and were much esteemed for their kindness and hospitality.

Our time was fully and pleasantly occupied by selecting the numerous articles required for establishing our Indian household, including a staff of servants.

Among other things we bought a handsome park-phaeton with a pair of chestnut cobs, and also a charger.

After a month's pleasant sojourn we took a cordial leave of our hospitable friends, and proceeded by steamer to Kurrachee, where my regiment was stationed. Arriving there in about three days, we were kindly welcomed by the Colonel and my brother officers. Here also we were fortunate in finding-kind friends to receive us till we secured an upper-storeyed bungalow and settled down there.

It was about seventeen years since I first landed there, when Sir Charles Napier was Governor and Commander-in-Chief in Scinde.

CHAPTER 17

India Again and Promotion

On our arrival at Kurrachee I was very glad to find that my old commanding officer, now promoted to be Major-General. Sir R. Honner, K.C.B., was commanding the division. I lost no time in reporting myself and calling upon him. He received me cordially, and I had the pleasure of introducing my wife to him. His A.D.C., Captain Glasspoole, was a brother officer of mine in the Indian Rifles.

Hitherto my military duties had been almost exclusively confined to Indian troops, and now that I was appointed to a European regiment, where the rules and regulations as well as interior economy are materially different, I, in addition to my other regimental work, attended orderly-room daily to become acquainted with the same.

My regiment, now H.M. 109th Foot, was formerly the 3rd Bombay Europeans of the Indian Army, which did excellent service through the Central India campaign under Sir Hugh Rose (Lord Strathnairn), especially at the siege and capture of Jhansi, and he used to call them his *zouaves*, and mentioned some of the officers in his despatches, including the late Major Armstrong, whom he recommended for a Victoria Cross for his gallantry, but which the home authorities reduced to a Brevet Majority.

As this young regiment suffered much in that very trying campaign not only from war but also from the deadly sun (by sunstroke) at the hottest season of the year, many were invalided, so that when the regiment arrived at Kurrachee it was much reduced in numbers and strength. To remedy this state of affairs, the Government adopted a very clever expedient, for there was at this time in India a portion of the British German Legion, which had served in the Crimea, and who volunteered from the Cape during the great Mutiny. In recognition of their services, to this Jager Corps (as it was called) a bounty was offered and gladly accepted. A number amounting to fully a wing of a regiment volunteered with a proportion of their officers. Thus, by this clever *coup* the Government not only secured the services of a highly trained and excellent body of officers and men, but were saved the heavy expenses of sending these men back to the Cape and bringing out a large batch of raw, fresh recruits from home. So in this instance the Indian Government scored.

There was no doubt a good deal of friction when these *Jagers* (as the men called them) first joined, but they soon got on very well together; and it was very amusing to hear sometimes an Irish soldier endeavouring to converse with a Jager friend in broken German with a strong Irish brogue! We had also the advantage from that foreign element of having an excellent band, one of the best in India, and our German Choristers, who sang splendidly their popular national songs (*Volks Lied*), of an evening alternately with our band at the Government Gardens, were very highly appreciated.

One of the German officers, Lieutenant Oscar Schmidt, soon after joining the regiment was selected as Adjutant, and he proved an excellent one.

Not long after we had settled down we received the sad news of the death at Edinburgh of a younger brother of mine, who was a Captain in the Royal Artillery, a promising young officer and a general favourite. However, soon after, my dear wife presented me with a little daughter, which somewhat cheered our spirits.

Early in 1864 our Colonel went home on leave, and the command of the regiment devolved upon me.

Soon after I had assumed this responsibility, our half-yearly inspection took place, and the regiment received the highest encomiums from the General Commanding.

After I had held the command for some months, our Colonel offered to retire for a consideration, and after sundry negotiations his offer was accepted. This was specially fortunate for me, and at length in the autumn I had the great satisfaction of being gazetted as Lieutenant-Colonel of the regiment. We did not, however, hear this good news till after we had left Kurrachee and reached Aden, for which delectable station we were now under orders to relieve a wing of H.M. 95th there. It was General Raines, himself commanding the station, who most kindly first informed me in writing of my promotion to Lieutenant-Colonel.

Previous to our departure from Kurrachee, about September of the year 1864, the society there being desirous of showing their appreciation of our efforts to cater for the public amusements and our hospitality in throwing open our mess to a large number of honorary members, gave us a farewell ball, and also invited the men, women, and children of the regiment to a banquet. The affair, which was a great success, was closed by a display of fireworks. This unusual compliment to the men was doubtless chiefly owing to the treat which our excellent German choristers had afforded to the station. A representation of this interesting scene appeared in the *Illustrated London News.*

After detaching three companies of the regiment to Hyderabad, under command of the senior Major, the headquarters of the regiment under my command embarked for Aden in the steamer *Coromandel.* After a week's fair passage we arrived there, and landing with as little delay as possible, marched to the Crater Camp, about four miles off, and relieved the wing of the 95th, who took our places in the same steamer to return to India.

The station of Aden is simply the crater of an extinct volcano, the most dismal and uninviting place possible, being surrounded on all sides by bare volcanic hills and without a particle of vegetation visible.

The houses, with one or two exceptions, were wretched, mere wattle-and-daub affairs, infested by rats, and their thatched roofs were quite inadequate for protection, as we found to our cost on one occasion when a heavy thunderstorm came on (an unusual occurrence) and the rain poured down through the roof like a sieve, so that we had to wade through the rooms with galoshes and an umbrella over our heads! Moreover, the accommodation for officers was scanty, but the men had excellent barracks, and were better off than we were.

These Somali Arabs are notorious thieves, against whom we were warned, one of their plans being to get one of their number engaged as a servant, and through his aid to gain access to the house.

An attempt was made on our house, which was frustrated by the vigilance of our little terrier, who subsequently, poor doggie! was poisoned by these wretches.

Aden, from its geographical position commanding the entrance of the Red Sea, is a place of great strategical and political importance, and from its strong and extensive fortifications, mounting several Armstrong guns, has good claim to be styled The Gibraltar of the East.

This military station is divided into three parts, viz., Steamer Point, The Isthmus, and Crater Camp.

At the first named reside the Political Agent, the General Commanding, and a certain proportion of troops. It is decidedly the most desirable position of the station, as the constant succession of mail and other steamers and vessels affords many opportunities of meeting with friends homeward or outward bound; it is, therefore, more gay and lively. The entrance to the Crater Camp, where my headquarters were, is through a tunnel cut out of the solid rock, and here also a native infantry regiment was stationed and some artillery.

The principal objects of interest here are the splendid reservoirs, said to have been built originally by the Turks, of solid masonry, and capable of holding an immense quantity of water entirely dependent on its rainfall, which is scanty, so that only a certain number of gallons are allowed to each person, and for which, moreover, he has to pay as we do at home for milk!

Grain, fodder, and firewood have to be brought in from the interior by an arrangement with the Sultan of Lahej, who receives a subsidy from Government.

Soon after my arrival I met Mr. Rassam, the assistant to the Political Agent there (Sir William Mereweather), who was an Armenian by birth and a great Oriental linguist. He was sent on a mission, accompanied by two English officers, to the King Theodore of Abyssinia to endeavour to effect the release of some missionaries and others whom without cause the King had made close prisoners—a very risky and unpleasant duty, with the result that they also were imprisoned—hence the Abyssinian war, the defeat and death of this tyrant, the capture of his capital, and the release by us of the poor prisoners.

Some years afterwards I met in Scotland the young Prince, son of the late King Theodore, who was sent to England for his education and was under the charge of Captain Speedy, one of the tallest men I ever saw, being, I think, 6 ft. 7 in. in height.

Life at Aden for both officers and men, as may be readily conceived, was extremely dull and monotonous, in fact mere vegetation. In order to remedy this, as much as possible, we had recourse to occasional picnics, but principally to theatricals; and as the theatre was a mere barn, the men, among whom were many handy fellows of all trades, set to work to build a new theatre, on a plan drawn by one of the officers, who superintended and completed the same. We had several good actors among both officers and men, some of the latter being extremely clever at scene-painting, and they had also capital voices. The place was duly opened as The Prince of Wales' Theatre, with the performance of Weber's celebrated opera of *Der Freiscühtz*, which was a great success.

Early in April 1865 we proceeded to Marshag, a high rocky plateau about a mile and a half from camp, which was a kind of sanatorium, and cooler, being more open to the sea-breezes, as my dear wife required a change, both of us being also depressed by the loss of a dearly loved son, who only survived six months in this horrid climate, which is so trying, especially for children.

When the hot weather set in, we were visited by that terrible scourge—the cholera—a very serious matter at all times, but especially in so confined an area as Aden. It first broke out among our Isthmus detachment, and spread to our camp. Prompt measures were taken to check this evil, by removing and isolating the cases, and forming a cholera camp on Syra Hill, under the medical charge of our energetic Assistant-Surgeon. The officers visited the hospital to keep up the men's spirits and show them that they were not neglected, a matter of great importance in such cases, and the General himself came down and visited them.

All parades, drills, etc., ceased, and the men were allowed to amuse themselves by fishing, bathing, etc.

By this means, under providence, this terrible scourge gradually disappeared. We had, however, to deplore the loss of several non-commissioned officers and men, and especially of our excellent Assistant-Surgeon (Dr. Nicol Carter), who fell a victim to the zealous discharge of his duties, and the General issued a special order in appreciation of the same. He was much esteemed, and his funeral was attended by nearly all the garrison.

Several of the natives died of this disease, including one of my regimental *peons*, or messengers, who, when bringing me a note from my adjutant, fell down when he reached my door, and being conveyed to the hospital, died soon afterwards. One of my own servants was also attacked, but a strong dose of chlorodyne and brandy being promptly, by my directions, administered to him, he recovered.

Unfortunately, during this trying time and the depressing effects of the climate, some of the men took to drinking heavily, and contracted a disease called *birbiree*, which caused a swelling of limbs

like dropsy, and several died from it. It was a sad and anxious time for me, especially as commanding officer.

However, as the weather got cooler, we returned to camp, and at the General's suggestion we got up various athletic sports, cricket, races, fencing, and single-stick exercises, at which last the Germans were very expert, and prizes were subscribed for by the officers, including the General, and some ladies kindly graced with their presence these Isthmian Games, as they were called, being carried on at the Isthmus Post.

For some time great difficulty and much inconvenience had arisen in procuring supplies from the interior, owing to the Arab tribes constantly attacking the caravans and carrying off the camels, etc. In fact, they showed such a refractory and defiant spirit, even sending threatening and insolent messages to H.M.'s Political Agent, that it was deemed necessary to chastise them, and thus give a severe lesson to these unruly Arab tribes.

Accordingly, in December 1865, a compact Field Force, consisting of a company of royal artillery with two Armstrong guns, a company of sappers and miners, three hundred European infantry of my regiment under Major Valentine, and a wing of the 1st Bombay Grenadiers Native Infantry, was formed, the whole being under the command of General Raines, C.B., while I, during his absence, was left in temporary command of the Aden garrison.

This Field Force advanced into the interior of Arabia, capturing and destroying several villages and small forts belonging to the refractory Arab tribes. The troops so frightened and harassed the enemy as to compel them to sue for peace and to give hostages for their future better behaviour. Altogether, the expedition was a most successful one, and the General informed me that he was especially pleased with the good conduct and spirit of my men, which was very gratifying to me. Some of the officers brought back sundry trophies of this expedition, and the surgeon of my regiment presented me with a Hebrew MS. of part of the Old Testament (*Leviticus*), beautifully written on dressed leather, found in one of the houses. One of the officers made some spirited sketches of the various forts and villages captured, which subsequently appeared in the *Illustrated London News*.

I was told that my men being in high spirits at their success used to sing on their return home their fine national songs, which were highly appreciated, as it tended to relieve the monotony of the march.

On the 30th November (St. Andrew's Day) 1865 another dear son was born to us at Aden.

I cannot conclude this record of our fifteen months' exile at Aden without referring to what may be looked upon as the red letter day of whole period—the occasion of the presentation of new colours to my regiment.

This interesting ceremony took place on the 23rd January 1866, in the presence of the elite of the station, and it went off with great *éclat*.

At my invitation, Mrs. Raines (now Lady Raines), the wife of our General, Sir J. Raines, G.C.B., assisted by my wife, presented the new colours, accompanied by a neat and graceful speech, after the colours had been consecrated by the chaplain, and were received with presented arms. In reply, I thanked her in the name of the regiment for her kind expressions, and added that though it was the youngest regiment of H.M.'s service, yet it was second to none in loyalty and devotion to the Crown.

In the evening, after the termination of the official part

of the proceedings, a banquet was given to the station by the regiment at the Aden Tanks and Gardens, which were brilliantly illuminated with hundreds of variegated lamps and Chinese lanterns, and a grand display of fireworks, etc. Indeed, it was said that such a fête had never before been witnessed by the oldest inhabitant at Aden.

A very full and interesting account of all these gala doings appeared in a Bombay paper, written, I believe, by some lady of literary taste.

My health having latterly been impaired, I was recommended by our surgeon to go home for further medical advice. Accordingly, I obtained a medical certificate to Europe, and though this step entailed considerable pecuniary loss, yet where health was concerned I had no hesitation.

On the 18th March 1866, after a farewell regimental dinner at the mess, and with many expressions of regret and regard from the regiments and other friends, we left without regret this dreary and barren spot—O joyful sound!—Homeward bound!

We left Aden on the 18th March 1866 by one of the P. and O. steamers for Suez, on by rail to Alexandria, and thence by French steamer, skirting the Grecian Archipelago, to Brindisi. On landing, we went by rail to Ancona, on the Adriatic, and in due course arrived at fair Florence. It was indeed a marvellous and delightful transformation and contrast between the barren and dreary desert we had quitted only a fortnight before, and this beautiful city, with its profusion of lovely flowers, green meadows, and shady trees of the Cascine, which we fully appreciated.

This change, combined with the warm greetings of old friends, speedily revived our spirits.

After a short stay in Florence we went direct to London, and arrived there about the end of April.

Soon after, I appeared before the Medical Board, and was granted a year's leave on sick certificate.

I was recommended by the medical authorities to undergo a serious operation, which I am thankful to say was successfully performed by an eminent surgeon.

The summer and winter of 1866 we spent principally and pleasantly in Scotland with my family. Although my health had on the whole improved, yet for various reasons I decided, after mature reflection, to retire from active service, provided the regiment agreed to my terms, which they did.

A Last Farewell

In the latter end of 1889 I was warmly invited by my son-in-law, Mr, S. M. Phraser of the Indian Civil Service, and my dear and only daughter, to pay them a visit in their Indian home, and to be introduced to my infant grandson. This invitation I accepted, and secured a three months' tour ticket.

I left London on the 21st November, being-accompanied to the P. & O. steamer *Clyde* by my wife and several friends, who gave us a good send-off. I was also escorting my niece who was going on a visit to her married sister in India. There were about one hundred and sixty passengers, and among them was an American gentleman who had been four times round the world! and was full of amusing anecdotes.

The *Clyde,* though a fine vessel, bore the unenviable character of being a roller, and this I found to my cost in the Bay of Biscay, where we encountered some very heavy seas. When crossing the deck the vessel rolled so fearfully that by a sudden lurch I was driven violently against an iron stanchion, which struck me on the side of the head, causing me to fall bleeding on the deck. Perhaps this accident may have been providential, as otherwise the impetus with which I was driven into the scuppers was so great that I might have lost my balance, and fallen overboard, as happened to the late Sir Howard Elphinstone, who thus lost his life some years ago. The doctor said it was a bad accident, and that I must remain quiet in my cabin for some days, and I took care not to alarm my niece.

Touching at Gibraltar and Malta we arrived at Port Said on the 5th December. This town has not got a good reputation, but it is important from its position at the entrance of the Suez Canal. It has a fine lighthouse, with a very powerful revolving electric light which, it is said, can be seen for thirty miles.

Entering the canal, we reached Ismailia, the head of the Sweet-Water Canal, with rail communication to Cairo. This was the landing-place and base of operations of Lord Wolseley's force in the Egyptian war, whence he made his celebrated night march, and stormed the entrenchments at Tel-el-Kebir, defeating the Egyptian army, and bringing this brilliant war to a close by the capture of Cairo!

Passing by Suez we steamed rapidly down the Red Sea to Aden. Unfortunately we arrived there at night, too late for me to go to my old quarters at the Crater Camp four miles off, and revisit the grave of our dear little son—much to my regret. This I hope to do, however, on my way back.

Leaving this Gibraltar of the East we arrived at Bombay on the 16th December 1889.

On anchoring, Colonel Luckhardt, C.B., A.D.C., Commissary General, an old brother officer of mine, from whose house my daughter was married, came on board. We greeted each other warmly, and arranged to meet later on at his house at Poona.

Bombay has progressed wonderfully since I saw it a quarter of a century before; and the group of handsome public buildings of carved grey stone facing the esplanade are splendidly imposing; and my Yankee globe-trotting friend pronounced it "the finest city in the Far East," with its tram-cars, electric light, and even skating rink and switch-back railway!

We remained here a few days to give my niece an opportunity of seeing something of this fine city, and also to secure for her a very good Portuguese servant who spoke English, as well as one of the same nationality for myself.

After seeing my niece off by rail to Saugor to visit her sister, the wife of Colonel M'Neill, on the 19th December, I proceeded by rail to Poona, and on arrival there, after taking a look round at this favourite station where I was quartered at one time, I took tiffin with Colonel and Mrs. Luckhardt and family, and was very glad to renew my acquaintance with them, and have a pleasant chat over old times.

Taking a cordial leave of them I went by the night train for Dharwar, passing through Sattara (first station in 1844) and on to the fine cantonment of Belgaum to Dharwar, where I arrived on the 21st, exactly a month after my leaving London. I was here cordially greeted by my dear daughter and son-in-law, and carried off in triumph. I lost no time in being introduced to my infant grandson, whom I found to be a remarkably jolly, engaging little fellow, of whom his parents had reason to be proud. We soon became great friends, and he used to come every morning with his mother or *ayah* to pay his *salaams* to his grandpapa, and have a little romp together.

At the request of the little mother a photograph was taken of us, he sitting on my knee, and the result was pronounced a great success. This young gentleman is now at Rugby—a stalwart youth, preparing for Sandhurst, to follow the profession of his grandfather in the Indian Army.

Dharwar, the capital of the district of that name, is a small Civil station, with no troops stationed there. It is quiet, cool, and healthy, and not far distant are the Daudelly Jungles, where there is fine big game shooting. My son-in-law holds here an appointment in the political department, being tutor and governor of H.H. the Maharajah of Kolapore and another native Prince of Bownuggur, to both of whom I was introduced. A former ruler of Kolapore and a near relative of the above visited England several years ago, and the handsome Kolapore Challenge Cup was presented by him to the nation for annual rifle competition. When travelling on the Continent he died at Florence, was cremated, and a fine marble and alabaster monument has been erected there to his memory at the Cascine. They are intelligent and studious, and the former was present in London at the Diamond Jubilee of our late gracious Queen, and received the decoration of G.C.S.I. (Grand Cross of the Star of India). Mr. Fraser who received from the King himself the Companion of the Indian Empire decoration, was also guardian and tutor to H.H. the Maharajah of Mysore; subsequently he was appointed by Lord Curzon, his officiating foreign secretary, and now holds the important influential post of Resident Political Agent to the Court of Mysore, at Bangalore, where he recently entertained Their Royal Highnesses the Prince and Princess of Wales.

The principal place of rendezvous is the gymkhana, which is the reading-room, well supplied with newspapers, a billiard table, and with lawn tennis and badminton courts adjoining. The European society is very limited, consisting of a few government officials, the collector, chaplain, civil surgeon; and the place is the headquarters of the Southern Mahratta Railway Company, with their employes and families, and a sprinkling of visitors.

On Christmas Day we attended divine service in the pretty little chapel, which was tastefully decorated, and we partook together of the Holy Communion with thankful hearts.

My son-in-law and others congratulated me on my not having forgotten the Indian language after so long an interval as a quarter of a century, which I attribute to the fact that I heard it spoken on all sides; moreover, the familiar scenes and sights around me, and their associations, revived in my mind what was lying dormant there, for I am sure, if I had remained still in England, I should have found some difficulty in carrying on a consecutive conversation in that lingo. This is, I think, a curious and interesting psychological fact.

The time of my departure had now come, so after taking affectionate leave of my dear relatives and others, with whom I had spent a pleasant month, I, on the 16th January 1890, left for

Belgaum where I was quartered forty years ago, and looked up my old bungalow at this beautiful and favourite station.

Being desirous of varying my route homewards I left Belgaum the following day, and proceeded by rail over the Braganza Ghaut, of which the scenery is very fine, to Goa, and was met at the terminus by Captain Oliver, the British Consul there, who kindly invited me to his house, which was most picturesquely situated across the harbour, with a delightful sea view. His wife is a handsome, charming lady, the daughter of Colonel Sartorius, V.C., of Burmese war distinction.

On the 20th January 1890, I took leave of my kind host and hostess, and proceeded by coast steamer to Bombay, where I arrived late the following day, and was the guest of some friends, living in their fine house at Breach Candy, which is furnished in the English style, with European furniture, papered walls, and gas in the bedrooms, and is the most Europeanised bungalow I have seen in India. This was a great novelty to me, as we military have nothing like it in our stations.

It was a singular coincidence that the house my friends previously occupied in Bombay (Belmont) was the one in which my dear daughter's mother was born, and where her parents lived for some time.

My final visit, before leaving India for the last time, was appropriately paid to my old Indian regiment, which happened by good fortune to be then quartered at Bombay. It is now styled H.M. Wellesley Rifles, from the fact that it served under the great Duke at the siege and storm of Seringapatam. When I joined the regiment our venerable Subahdar-Major (Suliman-Israel, of Hebrew descent) was the only man in it who had been present at that memorable siege, and was about to take his pension, having also received the highest decoration, the Order of British India. He was much esteemed, was an excellent officer, and very gentlemanly in appearance.

I called on the Commanding Officer, who asked me to dine at the mess, but finding that there was not a single officer there with the regiment who had been with me, while those senior to me had all passed away, and joined the great majority, I felt it would only revive sad memories, and therefore declined; I, however, went to see the regiment at drill, and was pleased to note the progress made, and more attention paid to shooting. I also much liked the new dress for the Native Army, which was more rational, like the *Zouaves*, and more in harmony with Oriental tastes, as well as more becoming and comfortable. The men wore knickerbockers with gaiters, and khaki coats and *pugree*, or turban, instead of a cap, my regiment having a rifle, green-dyed coat, and green turban with red tuft. I conversed with some of the native officers and men, inquiring for various members, and found all I knew were either dead or pensioned, among them being my old Quarter-Master Sergeant, Daniel-Israel, who was also the Rabbi of his tribe in the regiment. They seemed much gratified at my looking them up, and coming all the way from England to see the old *Pultun* regiment, and I took a cordial leave of them. The centenary of my regiment occurred in the year 1888 at Bombay, when Lieutenant-Colonel Sir W. Seton, Bart., was in command, and was an interesting event in the history of the regiment.

On the 24th January 1890, after taking leave of my hospitable friends, I embarked aboard the fine P. & O. steamer *Ganges,* and bade adieu to India for the last time, casting a lingering look behind as we steamed rapidly out to sea. May God bless India, and hasten the time when her people shall throw off the dark cloud of idolatry and superstition, which has hung for ages, like a pall, over the land, and yield allegiance to the Lord Jesus Christ.

We arrived at Aden on the 29th, again unfortunately too late at night to visit the old Crater Camp. Here I received welcome letters from home.

The officers of this mail steamer have a very ingenious way of keeping their cabins cool, by means of wire rods attached to their punkahs, and communicating with the piston or rod of the engine, which is kept in constant motion, thus dispensing with manual aid, and keeping their cabins constantly cool. I may also mention that each P. & O. steamer has an ice-room for keeping the meat fresh, which was a great luxury.

We reached Suez on the 3rd February, and passing through the Canal we duly arrived at Port Said. I at once made inquiries there from the obliging agent of Messrs. Grindlay & Co., as to whether there were any parties *en route* to the Holy Land, as this place is only fifteen hours by steam from Jaffa (the ancient Joppa), but was informed there were none there, nor any expected, being rather early in the season, so here again I was disappointed, for I could not stay in this evil place for an indefinite time.

Pazienza, there seems a fatality about my visiting the Holy Land, which has been the dream of my life, and for which I have had an intense desire. On one occasion in the spring, when I was arranging about going, I was taken ill, another time I was suffering from cataract, and on the third occasion I had actually got my ticket to go with Bishop Perowne's party, and had sent off my luggage, when I learnt that my only surviving sister was dangerously ill in Scotland, and wished to see me, so I had reluctantly to give the journey up altogether.

Among the passengers we picked up at Ismailia was Captain Nelson, one of Stanley's intrepid staff, who accompanied him in his wonderful march through Africa to the successful relief of Emin Pasha, and he gave me an interesting account of the same.

After leaving Port Said we encountered rougher weather in the Mediterranean than we had hitherto had, and after landing the mails at Brindisi proceeded to Malta, arriving there on the 9th.

On landing in company with a friend we climbed up to a terrace through a gateway adorned with medieval figures of the Knights Templars; we had a splendid panoramic view of the harbour crowded with shipping, and the city, which was *en fête,* gaily decorated in honour of San Paulo, the patron Saint of Malta. In the evening there were illuminations and a display of fireworks.

Quitting Malta we duly arrived at *Gib* where I also landed in company with a young lady, and took a stroll through the main street and bazaar, making some purchases. We visited the *alameda* or public gardens, where the band plays, examined with interest the Woolwich Infant (a hundred-ton-gun) a huge monster, which is worked and cleaned by hydraulic power.

Leaving Gibraltar on the 12th, and passing Cadiz and Oporto we were off Cape Finisterre on the 14th, rolling heavily.

On Sunday, February 16th, we passed the Lizards and Eddystone Lighthouse, encountering the roughest weather we had experienced throughout, and arrived at Plymouth about 5 p.m. in a storm of rain and wind.

Leaving Plymouth on the afternoon of the 17th, and passing through lovely Devonshire, I arrived at Bournemouth about 8.30 p.m., and was warmly welcomed by my dear wife and family. *Grazia Dio,* for all His mercies in bringing me safe home. Altogether my trip was a great success and an enjoyable one.

Soon after my arrival at home, I learnt with much grief and sorrow that my dear and valued cousin, General J. Bellasis, had passed away on the 10th March 1890, in his eighty-third year. We were a good deal together in India, and he was present with me at the siege of Mooltan, and I had a great regard for him, as he was very kind to me throughout his life. Peace be to his memory. *Riposa in Pace.*

In the spring of 1892 I received an invitation from my regiment, then at Aldershot, to visit them, which I accepted, and received a cordial welcome. After lunch at the mess, and being introduced to the officers new to me, I called on the General Commanding (Sir Evelyn Wood, with whom I had served during the Indian Mutiny) and also inspected the regiment. Since the system of double-linked battalions has been adopted by the Government, my regiment is now styled the 2nd Battalion, the Prince of Wales's Leinster Regiment (Royal Canadians), thus representing not only an Irish province, but also the great Dominion of Canada, in which country I feel a special interest, my family from the maternal side having been closely connected with it. One of my uncles, the late Lieutenant H. Armstrong of the Canadian Fencible Regiment, was killed in action during the war of 1812, in defence of his country, and another, the late General R, Armstrong, R.A., who served throughout the war, was wounded, and had two horses shot under him at the capture of Fort Erie, Buffalo, etc.; after upwards of fifty-four years' service he received a distinguished service pension. My only son, Mr. Frederick Armstrong Maude, is well acquainted with Canada, having been partly educated at the Guelph Agricultural College, and he is the sole survivor and representative of that family bearing their name.

I subsequently had the pleasure and privilege of presiding at the annual regimental dinner, held in London on the 3rd June 1892, but alas! there were few of my brother-officers left who had served with me in India.

About this time Lord Roberts visited Bournemouth and was entertained by the municipal authorities, when I had the pleasure of being introduced to him.

The Indian Army has reason to be proud of its history, from the time of the daring and dauntless Lord Clive who may be said to have founded our Indian Empire, and the able soldier-statesman, Sir John Malcolm, who consolidated it, down to that noble Christian soldier, Henry Lawrence, the hero of Lucknow, the chivalrous Outram, the able Herbert Edwardes who guarded the frontier, the heroic Nicholson of Delhi fame, and last, but not least, this distinguished soldier, Lord Roberts, who by his skilful tactics may be said to have saved the situation in South Africa, and is now in the evening of his life endeavouring patriotically to rouse his countrymen, in these critical times, to the supreme importance of universal military training of our youth and manhood, and has thereby earned the gratitude of his country.

In bringing to a close these records of my varied and not uneventful life, amid the pine-clad woods of lovely Bournemouth, enjoying ease and comfort under my own roof-tree *(sub tegmine pini)* surrounded by my family and grandchildren, I feel I owe a deep debt of gratitude to the Almighty, "Giver of every good and perfect gift," for His many mercies to me and mine, in preserving me through many and great dangers, and bringing me safe home, in reasonably good health at the age of fourscore years, and also the Doyen and sole survivor of forty-two grandchildren of our branch of the family.

Surely, then, I may well exclaim, "O Lord, who lendeth me life, give me a heart replete with thankfulness"; and I can conclude in no more fitting words than those of the inspired Psalmist, "Bless the Lord, O my soul, and forget not all His benefits; who healeth all thy diseases, forgiveth all thine iniquities, and who crowneth thee with loving kindness and tender mercies."

POSTSCRIPT

In closing these *Memoirs*, I may mention that I was present by invitation at the great banquet to our Indian Mutiny veterans in London. It was a touching and pathetic sight to inspect these poor war-worn fellows on this their last muster parade on earth! It is a cause of thankfulness that something is at last being done for their future welfare and comfort, and not to let them die in a workhouse and fill a pauper's grave. *E. M.*

LEONAUR
ALSO FROM LEONAUR
AVAILABLE IN SOFTCOVER OR HARDCOVER WITH DUST JACKET

THE JENA CAMPAIGN: 1806 *by F. N. Maude*—The Twin Battles of Jena & Auerstadt Between Napoleon's French and the Prussian Army.

PRIVATE O'NEIL *by Charles O'Neil*—The recollections of an Irish Rogue of H. M. 28th Regt.—The Slashers— during the Peninsula & Waterloo campaigns of the Napoleonic wars.

ROYAL HIGHLANDER *by James Anton*—A soldier of H.M 42nd (Royal) Highlanders during the Peninsular, South of France & Waterloo Campaigns of the Napoleonic Wars.

CAPTAIN BLAZE *by Elzéar Blaze*—Elzéar Blaze recounts his life and experiences in Napoleon's army in a well written, articulate and companionable style.

LEJEUNE VOLUME 1 *by Louis-François Lejeune*—The Napoleonic Wars through the Experiences of an Officer on Berthier's Staff.

LEJEUNE VOLUME 2 *by Louis-François Lejeune*—The Napoleonic Wars through the Experiences of an Officer on Berthier's Staff.

FUSILIER COOPER *by John S. Cooper*—Experiences in the 7th (Royal) Fusiliers During the Peninsular Campaign of the Napoleonic Wars and the American Campaign to New Orleans.

CAPTAIN COIGNET *by Jean-Roch Coignet*—A Soldier of Napoleon's Imperial Guard from the Italian Campaign to Russia and Waterloo.

FIGHTING NAPOLEON'S EMPIRE *by Joseph Anderson*—The Campaigns of a British Infantryman in Italy, Egypt, the Peninsular & the West Indies During the Napoleonic Wars.

CHASSEUR BARRES *by Jean-Baptiste Barres*—The experiences of a French Infantryman of the Imperial Guard at Austerlitz, Jena, Eylau, Friedland, in the Peninsular, Lutzen, Bautzen, Zinnwald and Hanau during the Napoleonic Wars.

MARINES TO 95TH (RIFLES) *by Thomas Fernyhough*—The military experiences of Robert Fernyhough during the Napoleonic Wars.

HUSSAR ROCCA *by Albert Jean Michel de Rocca*—A French cavalry officer's experiences of the Napoleonic Wars and his views on the Peninsular Campaigns against the Spanish, British And Guerilla Armies.

SERGEANT BOURGOGNE *by Adrien Bourgogne*—With Napoleon's Imperial Guard in the Russian Campaign and on the Retreat from Moscow 1812 - 13.

www.ingramcontent.com/pod-product-compliance
Lightning Source LLC
Chambersburg PA
CBHW021110090426
42738CB00006B/588